D1236844

D/

THINKING
IN THE RUINS

THE VANDERBILT LIBRARY OF AMERICAN PHILOSOPHY

Other titles in the series include

THINKING
IN THE
RUINS

Wittgenstein and Santayana on Contingency

MICHAEL HODGES AND JOHN LACHS

VANDERBILT UNIVERSITY PRESS
NASHVILLE

First Edition 2000

04 03 02 01 00   5 4 3 2 1

Library of Congress Cataloging-in-Publication Data

Hodges, Michael P.
  Thinking in the ruins : Wittgenstein and Santayana on
contingency / Michael Hodges and John Lachs. — 1st ed.
    p. cm. — (The Vanderbilt library of American philosophy)
  Includes bibliographical references and index.
  ISBN 0-8265-1341-7 (alk. paper)
  1. Wittgenstein, Ludwig, 1889–1951. 2. Santayana, George,
1863–1952. I. Lachs, John. II. Title. III. Series.
  B3376.W564 H63 2000
  191—dc21   99-6700

Published by Vanderbilt University Press
Printed in the United States of America

Contents

Series Editor's Preface   vii
Preface   x
Abbreviations   xiii

1   Thinking in the Ruins   1
2   Displacing Skepticism   15
3   The Contingency of Values   35
4   Forms of Life and Animal Faith   55
5   Religious Belief   70
6   Conclusion   87

Notes   109
Bibliography   119
Index   124

Series Editor's Preface

Wittgenstein and Santayana are not philosophers one naturally thinks of as similar, but one should. The similarities begin in biography and importance. Both are significant philosophers in the development of Western thought. By most lights Wittgenstein is regarded as one of the most influential philosophers of the twentieth century, and Santayana is considered as a major philosopher, poet, and cultural critic. They were contemporaries whose friendships and pathways crisscrossed several times, although there is no evidence of direct contact between them. Had they met and discussed philosophy, the discovery of their common outlooks might be less dramatic than it is. Their personal lives and philosophies highlight significant fin de siècle themes as well as the authentic search for beginnings in a new century. Each wrote his mature philosophy during a time of remarkable development and ruination in the Western world. Each found solace in philosophical reflection apart from the bustling energy of business enterprise, athletics, and social activity. And, perhaps with startling surprise, each came to very similar conclusions regarding major philosophical questions of the day. Furthermore they were prescient, responding to issues that are now at the forefront of consideration, and their responses are in a style and elegance more striking and thoughtful than most philosophical approaches to the same issues.

The congruence of Wittgenstein's and Santayana's thought has been overlooked, blatantly overlooked, and recent research on both philosophers makes their philosophical and cultural similarities all the more salient. In 1963 Arthur Danto wrote that many philosophers are recapitulating "the intellectual crisis which Santayana helped overcome," breaking through "to a view of things not dissimilar to the one he [Santayana] achieved" ("Santayana and the Task Ahead," *Nation*, 21 December 1963, 437–40). Lachs and Hodges follow Danto's invitation to reexamine Santayana's thought, and their work has the added benefit of knowledge gained through the Wittgenstein and Santayana critical editions as well as recent intellectual biographies on both philosophers. The significance of this volume is also highlighted by its aptness for understanding postmodernist philosophy and its alternatives.

Each philosopher has a distinctive writing style that confounds the problem of comparison. Santayana is more literate. He artistically crafts his positions with historical allusions and careful clarity. Wittgenstein's work is more enigmatic, sometimes only adumbrating carefully thought-out positions. His knowledge of the history of philosophy has been underplayed. In part the differences in styles explain why their intellectual agreements have been hidden from previous studies. Presently the work of both is undergoing reexamination and evaluation. This volume is a major step in achieving a better understanding of the pivotal role of each philosopher and how they found a similar vector and destination for their philosophical outlooks.

Once one is beyond their differences in literary and philosophical style, their parallel approaches and conclusions are both apparent and remarkable. Their rejections of skepticism have a similar base, and their responses to skepticism appear almost identical. Santayana's concept of animal faith consistently parallels Wittgenstein's references to a conviction or belief as "beyond being justified or unjustified; as it were, as something animal" (Wittgenstein, *On Certainty*, 359). And Wittgenstein's focus on "forms of life" and human practices parallels Santayana's focus on the capaciousness of social and cultural practices articulated institutionally, on the unconscious physical complexity of individual and social action, and on the depths of individual suffering, joy, and responsibility.

The Vanderbilt Library of American Philosophy series explores the historical roots of American thought as well its cutting edges. This volume examines two major figures in Western thought. One, Santayana, is clearly American in education and philosophical outlook although he retained his Spanish citizenship throughout his life. The other, Wittgenstein, is American in neither background nor outlook. In actuality both Santayana and Wittgenstein are world philosophers, not national or parochial in perspective. The intellectual wedding of these two philosophers highlights the centrality of themes in American thought and their centrality to philosophical concerns on any continent. For

Series Editor's Preface

Santayana, one of the foremost Hispanic-American thinkers, the intellectual nexus with Wittgenstein draws American thought into the wider range of philosophical concerns, something that would please Santayana.

Santayana's often repeated epigram is worth noting: those who cannot remember the past are condemned to repeat it. The overlooked likenesses between Santayana and Wittgenstein may be understandable given philosophical styles and trends, but it is not excusable. Examining the comparabilities of their philosophies provides a genuine advancement in historical and contemporary understanding-an advancement worth noting and remembering.

Herman J. Saatkamp, Jr.

Preface

Our topic is the striking, and hitherto unsuspected, similarity between the thought of Wittgenstein and the philosophy of Santayana. The kinship is disguised by differences of language and philosophical approach. One of the dissimilarities makes for an unavoidable asymmetry in the presentation of our material.

The later Wittgenstein, who, with the later, ontologically explicit Santayana, is the object of our investigation, assiduously avoids straightforward statements of his philosophical position. His composition sidesteps exposition, consisting instead of epigrammatic remarks, marginal reflections, and the questions and answers of imagined conversations. The significance of his comments is not always easy to divine; sometimes one cannot even be sure which voice in the fragmentary dialogues is meant to be his own. We shall argue that this is not perversity on Wittgenstein's part but rather a function of the way he sees philosophy.

Santayana, by contrast, is at pains to state his philosophical position explicitly. Though encumbered by scholastic terminology, he spends considerable effort in clarifying the ways in which his use of such terms as "substance" and "essence" differs from that of his predecessors. He situates his ideas by comparing them with the views of major thinkers from Plato to Russell and states them again and again to achieve unmistakable clarity.

This dissimilarity in their modes of presenting their positions has forced an asymmetry on our own presentation. Wittgenstein's views must be painstakingly pieced together from hints and comments throughout his posthumously published corpus. In our account of what he had in mind, some is conjecture, and much of the rest is interpretation. These are essential tools in the reconstruction of his ideas, which is the necessary first step in comparing them with Santayana's.

Our expositions of Wittgenstein's views are, accordingly, longer and more elaborate than those we provide for Santayana's. Quotations from

Preface

Wittgenstein serve as platforms on which our interpretations are built; quotations from Santayana, by contrast, are offered as useful illustrations of otherwise clear positions. Our hope is that the unequal allocation of space to our two thinkers has made it possible for us to pay equally conscientious attention to them.

Wittgenstein is a sufficiently enigmatic philosopher to have spawned schools of divergent interpretation. We cannot expect that everyone will agree with our reading of his thought. We do not think our task includes convincing Wittgenstein commentators everywhere that our interpretation is the only correct one or even that it is the best. We will have done enough if we do not misrepresent this difficult philosopher and if we can show that our view of him constitutes a plausible and productive reading.

Being a much more direct and less open-ended thinker, no such interpretive difficulties beset our account of Santayana. Even the great current revival of his thought has produced only richer and deeper appreciation of his ideas, not significantly divergent readings of them. We hope to add to this richness by showing unexpected connections between his views and what was going on concurrently in another part of Europe and in a vastly different tradition of thought.

Concerning the intriguing historical question of contact or direct influence between our two thinkers, we can offer only conjectures. From the 1890s on, Santayana was a regular visitor to Cambridge University. He had continuing, close personal contact with Bertrand Russell and was in intellectual touch with G. E. Moore. He was a voracious reader and made a point of scrutinizing (and often criticizing) the work of significant contemporaries. There can be no doubt that he read the *Tractatus Logico-Philosophicus*.

For more than twenty-five years after his retirement from Harvard in 1912, Santayana traveled in Europe. He continued to visit Cambridge and remained in vigorous correspondence with a number of philosophers. Though it is unlikely that he welcomed the development of British philosophy in the 1930s and 1940s, he was probably well aware of Wittgenstein's changed views and of his growing influence.

Wittgenstein's ignorance of the works of other philosophers has been much exaggerated. We know that he read Schopenhauer and James, both major influences on Santayana. He may well have read Santayana also, though we have no direct evidence of this. It is not at all impossible that the two met; there were plenty of occasions at Cambridge when

Preface

they could have been introduced to one another and spent some time conversing.

The possible personal connection is intriguing but in the end unimportant. What matters is that in their different idioms they articulated strikingly similar views. If we think of philosophies as responses not only to intellectual, but also to historical and social developments, this should not surprise us. Though superficially different, jonquils and tulips celebrate the spring under the influence of the same nurturing sun and rain. Wittgenstein and Santayana formed their mature views at a time when the comfortable certainties of Western civilization were crumbling all around them. What they say is similar at least in part because they wished to resist the spread of ruin by relying on the calm sanity of our established practices.

Chapter 1 of this book appeared in a slightly different form in *Overheard in Seville: Bulletin of the Santayana Society* 13 (Fall 1995): 1–8. We thank the National Endowment for the Humanities for the Collaborative Programs grant that made the writing of this book possible. It heartens us to note that philosophy need not be the private reflection of the isolated soul; the cooperation that has brought great results in science and social improvement may yet find its way into the humanities. We thank Thomas Crocker for help in preparing the endnotes and the bibliography. We thank our families for continuing support and wish to note our grateful appreciation of the tradition of philosophical reflection that has given us an inexhaustibly rich collection of imaginative views about virtually every topic of interest to the human mind.

Abbreviations

CV	*Culture and Value*
OC	*On Certainty*
IPR	*Interpretations of Poetry and Religion*
LC	*Lectures and Conversations*
PI	*Philosophical Investigations*
POML	*Physical Order and Moral Liberty*
RB	*Realms of Being*
RFGB	*Remarks on Frazer's Golden Bough*
RFM	*The Remarks on the Foundations of Mathematics*
RR	*Reason and Religion*
SAF	*Scepticism and Animal Faith*
WD	*Winds of Doctrine*

Chapter 1

THINKING IN THE RUINS

George Santayana and Ludwig Wittgenstein seem improbable candidates for comparative study, which may well be why no one has looked for similarities in their philosophical ideas. The two seem to be engaged in radically different projects. They appear to agree neither on their presuppositions and methods nor in their aims and results. Even their styles are divergent and their sensibilities incompatible.

The surprising reality, however, is that there are tantalizing similarities between the philosophical positions of Santayana and Wittgenstein. In the context of overwhelming apparent differences, the remarkable extent of these resemblances is adequate by itself to warrant investigation. But there also are other compelling philosophical reasons for looking at this relationship.

To understand the differences and the similarities between Santayana and Wittgenstein better, it is important to take a closer look at the time in which they lived. In the years between the two world wars, many began to feel that the intellectual, moral, religious and social traditions that had been in place for a long time were in ruins. The social structures of Victorian England were crumbling, and the progress of the Industrial Revolution had begot the horrors of modern warfare. Whereas F. H. Bradley had been able to write confidently about "My Station and Its Duties," a generation later Jean-Paul Sartre could find nothing but "bad faith" in a life of devotion to one's social role. The intellectual, moral, and religious practices that philosophers had attempted to justify by showing their ground in some transcending certainty came to seem arbitrary or suspended in thin air.

The First World War appeared to bring down every tradition and brought the downfall of empires that traced their heritage to the days of Rome. It also leveled the dominant intellectual tradition, which consisted of the search for certainty, a search that had defined the philosophical project at least from Descartes's day, and on some accounts from Plato's.[1] Philosophers who wrote under the influence of the war thought that, since human practices were in need of grounding and none could be provided, life was pervaded by uncertainty. They expressed these feelings of displacement and homelessness in the thought that nothing anyone had claimed to know could withstand criticism. Seeing only ruins, they maintained that actions could receive no justification and that lives, cut loose from any foundation, were meaningless. These thinkers saw empty contingency where necessity and certainty had been; their reaction took the form of skepticism about knowledge and values, and cynicism about life.

This "modern malaise" has been noted by many, though few have related it to philosophy. As a result, no one has noticed that the two figures with whom we are concerned, who flourished in those years and who went about the task of doing philosophy in strikingly different ways, nevertheless share remarkable similarities of thought and attitude. Santayana and Wittgenstein could well be viewed as philosophers of homelessness. Both were personally displaced and intellectually homeless. Santayana was a Spaniard who lived in the United States and later in Europe, but as an adult never in his land of birth. Wittgenstein was an Austrian who gave up his birthright— not only his country of birth but also his family inheritance—and lived out his life in England. He expressed his alienation from the modern vision of life in many places.[2] Santayana's disengaged, spectatorial stance was evident in his solitary life and in his philosophical view of the world as his "host" and of himself as a transient guest.

Perhaps it was this personal homelessness that made it possible for each in his own way to appreciate the character of the intellectual problems that emerged from the fragmentation of the modern world. In any case, the philosophical kinship between the two is as deep as it is surprising. Both responded to the modern condition not by delegitimating the practices in which our lives are expressed, but by discarding the traditional project of the search for certain foundations. In so doing, both struggled with and rejected skepticism.[3] This allowed them, in their different ways, to preserve a great deal of the tradition their age persisted in questioning. Each manifested a deep respect for the wisdom implicit in long-standing human practices and rejected as worthless and shallow any skepticism that failed to take into account the realities of the human situation.

By breaking with the requirement of certain foundations, Santayana and Wittgenstein were able to appreciate the integrity of human practices. According to both, it is not living human knowledge but a mistaken philosophical tradition that demands foundations and thus creates intellectual homelessness and displacement. Both thought that to get our house in order, we have to rethink our social, religious, philosophical, and moral practices outside the context of the search for certainty. This insight and the projects that flowed from it define the philosophical kinship of George Santayana and Ludwig Wittgenstein.

Here we shall focus on one aspect of our larger project of exploring the complex relations between the thought of Santayana and that of Wittgenstein: Santayana's and Wittgenstein's responses to the twentieth century's painful discovery of contingency. This is done best by putting their ideas in context and viewing them as two related, though interestingly different, approaches among historical alternatives.

The modern malaise had a variety of technological, social, economic, and political causes. Intellectually it came to consciousness as the recognition that our values and practices are thoroughly contingent, that they lack the certainty, rightness, or absolute justification prior generations insisted they could attain. The wrenching growth of this complex consciousness is what we call "the discovery of contingency." We do not mean to assert, of course, that thinkers in other ages had not been aware of the contingency of events, of the historical situatedness of our values and of the happenstance character of some of our most dearly held beliefs. But the upheavals of the twentieth century made it difficult even for ordinary people to believe in the privileged status of their own ways. Confronted with alternative modes of life, we face an unprecedented level of uncertainty about the practices and values that define us.

There are at least six distinct responses to the discovery of contingency. The traditional view is one of denial. This Cartesian-like move attempts to pull the sting of contingency by stressing a necessity that grounds or transcends it. Affirming the reality of eternal forms, self-evident necessary truths, God, the transcendental unity of apperception, and the Absolute Spirit are ways of responding to contingency that deny its ultimate hold on us.

Such approaches typically maintain that there is no *real* contingency: only if we cut ourselves off from "the ground of our being" can our lives and practices be seen as contingent. If, on the other hand, we view contingency against the backdrop of the necessary structures of being, thought, consciousness, or language, it loses its significance or simply disappears.

At the opposite pole, skeptics and nihilists embrace a message of desperation. The nihilist, as we use the term, accepts the demand for foundations but thinks we can find none. Thus our intellectual and moral practices are left suspended in midair. They may be inescapable in our situation, but they are tragically unjustified. Since questionable rules cannot provide reliable guidance, we face desperation or a permanent crisis.

The two poles of denying contingency and despairing at its universality define the outer limits of modern philosophy. The era began with Descartes's demand for absolute certainty and culminated in Nietzsche's withering assessment and ultimate displacement of such demands in favor of a play of forces understood as the "will to power."[4]

In the twentieth century at least four other ways of appropriating contingency were developed. Two of these are perhaps fairly well known; two others, those of Santayana and Wittgenstein, have not received adequate attention. The better-known responses are clearly exemplified in the works of Dewey and in the ideas of various so-called postmodern thinkers.

Let us consider Dewey first. For him the demand for foundations is itself illicit or compensatory. The quest for certainty is an understandable but unintelligent response to the need for security in a precarious world. Instead of seeking to improve our lot piecemeal or gradually, we want wholesale guaranties of the legitimacy and ultimate success of our enterprises. In doing so, we forget the context in which our practices have developed. To see these practices as contingent is not to see them as unjustified, but rather as historically specific responses to problematic situations. They represent solutions to problems that have plagued us. Because the problems may change and the solutions may not work for long, recognition of the contingency of our practices is at once acceptance of the need to adapt new means to old or novel ends.

The contingency of value thus opens the possibility of the sort of criticism and reconstruction that is characteristic of Dewey's pragmatism. All such criticism is itself rooted in values, but this creates no problem for Dewey. There are no absolute foundations, no fixed starting point from which all thinking must or should proceed. Rather we begin where we are and evaluate our situation in light of the values we happen to hold. The assessment continues or resumes each time we fail to achieve satisfaction. In the process, no value is free from criticism, and every value can be replaced or modified.

The key is to become aware of the conditions and consequences of living by or acting on particular values. In the light of these, we can intelligently modify or reject our allegiances. We may discover, for example, that the satisfaction of certain of our desires is incompatible with other established values. Or we may find that economic, social, or technological changes increase or lower the cost of satisfying some wants. Such changes call for specific and piecemeal adjustments to our values. There is no general rule as to how such adjustments should be made. We experiment and see if the results are satisfactory.

The point is that, for Dewey, values and the practices that go with them are neither absolute nor arbitrary. Every value can and may

sooner or later have to be questioned. But every practice is historically situated and was established to meet some human need. Some
of them, of course, have become so deeply entrenched that we cannot even imagine ourselves without them. Our lives and identities
may well depend on holding fast to such practices. Dewey does not
claim that every change is possible for everyone. But changes are en-
demic, and our homey comfort is constantly in the process of being
eroded. If we are lucky, the changes are gradual. And if we are intelligent, we may control them and so increase our satisfactions. We
have reason neither for assurance nor for despair. But a cautious
confidence in constructive action may well bring good results.

So far we have seen denial, despair, and acceptance with the hope
of amelioration as responses to contingency and homelessness. The
fourth response might well be called "postmodern." There is no fully
developed position of the sort we shall describe within the work of
any one thinker. But the composite picture gives a reasonably accurate representation of many features characteristic of the postmodern stance.

If anything can be central to an intellectual activity whose aim is
to decenter our practices, interruption of the normal is. Here contingency is embraced, if not actually flaunted: we are reminded again
and again that our normalized social structures and relations lack a
legitimating "metanarrative." But worse, as products of the Enlightenment, they supposedly participate in a nostalgia for unity and totality that amounts to the exclusion and destruction of whatever
exceeds them.

The power of our normal practices in claiming absolute authority
and justification is therefore dangerous. This power must be prob-
lematized: we must learn to experience our institutions as limited
and exclusionary and ourselves as homeless in relation to them.
Without such distancing or deferring, it is impossible to maintain a
critical edge. Without it a great deal of violence and terror go unno-
ticed or seem implicitly "justified" as simply a part of normal practice. Even the pursuit of solutions within the structure of our
practices merely continues in place the destructive if invisible fofces
of normalization. Painful as this is, we must retain an attitude of

suspicion and questioning. Only constant reminders of contingency can help us remember our practical and intellectual tendency to surrender to or to invent the absolute.

These varied responses to contingency help us understand some of the truly interesting features of the work of Wittgenstein and the thought of Santayana. With regard to human practices, at least, Wittgenstein appears to be deeply conservative. Throughout both the *Tractatus* and *Philosophical Investigations*,[5] one of his primary concerns is to prune the claims of philosophy either to support or to undermine our basic practices. Instead of formulating a direct response to contingency and its attendant feeling of homelessness, Wittgenstein undertakes to examine why the adventitious nature of our practices should bother us at all. His answer takes the form of a powerful indictment of philosophy.[6]

Traditional philosophical thought has viewed itself as the capping stone of the human cognitive enterprise. Consequently it has created the impression that our religious, ethical, and epistemic practices require a foundation that only it, with its access to certainty, can provide. Without such grounding, the practices supposedly lack legitimacy, and we can never be sure that what we do is defensible or right.

Such an approach to contingency and to the task of philosophy constitutes, for Wittgenstein, a radical mistake. A primary purpose of his later work is to expose the pretensions of philosophy by showing, among other things, the discontinuity between philosophical problems and our actual practices. The "philosopher's trick" is to convince us that the philosophical uses of such terms as "reason," "doubt," and "knowledge" are somehow continuous with or even underlie our ordinary employment of them. Nothing could be farther from the truth, Wittgenstein believes, and he proceeds to unmask the pretensions of this pompous but hollow mode of thought.

In the *Philosophical Investigations* he tries to show that philosophy has nothing positive to contribute; it "leaves everything as it is." Our practices are not grounded in any philosophical foundation, and they lack nothing if they fail to live up to the demand for certainty. Everything is in order just as it is. He affirms this not only when he writes about epistemic matters, but also when he discusses religious belief in such works as *Culture and Value* and *Remarks on Frazer's Golden Bough*.[7] In the latter, he argues that Frazer misconceived the nature of religious belief by assimilating it to scientific or pseudoscientific claims.[8] Thus Frazer's arguments for rejecting religion in favor of science fall short or, worse, miss the point. Religious beliefs are not primitive scientific convictions to be replaced by new cognitive developments. In *Culture and Value,* he goes so far as to reject the need even for a historical foundation of Christianity.[9] "Queer as it sounds: The historical accounts in the Gospels might, historically speaking, be demonstrably false and yet belief would lose nothing by this: not, however, because it concerns 'universal truths of reason'! Rather, because historical proof (the historical proof-game) is irrelevant to belief . . ." (p. 32). The language-game of religious belief is not to be confused with history or with science or with that of "truths of reason," whatever those might be. Rather it is sui generis; "It is just another language-game" (*PI,* 64). As such, it is not open to question and criticism from any extraneous direction. Everything is in order just as it is.[10]

But if everything *is* in order, then we are free to "relax into" our institutions—to accept our form of life, as Wittgenstein might have said. This almost stoic position is expressed clearly in a comment from 1946. "If life becomes hard to bear we think of a change in our circumstances. But the most important and effective change, a change in our own attitude, hardly even occurs to us, and the resolution to take such a step is very difficult for us" (*CV,* p. 53).[11] What makes us feel uneasy is not that our practices are, from some cosmic standpoint, contingent, but the illusion created by traditional philosophy's demand for foundations. Once such demands are quieted, we can with good conscience feel at home with what we have.

This conservative response arises at least in part out of distrust of the idea of "progressive transformation" that underlies industrial life and philosophical positions similar to Dewey's. It is, moreover, sharply at odds with the suspicions, the interruptions, and the ceaseless questionings of postmodern thinkers.[12] Wittgenstein sees himself as resisting what he calls the "main current of European and

American civilization" with its devotion to progress. He is bothered by the fact that everything is supposed to accomplish something. "Even clarity," he says, "is sought only as a means to an end, not as an end in itself. For me on the contrary clarity, perspicuity are valuable in themselves" (*CV*, pp. 6–7). Philosophy itself has a finite, nonprogressive task: it comes to an end once we "command a clear view of the use of our words" (*PI*, 122). After all, "Philosophy may in no way interfere with the actual use of language; it can in the end only describe it. For it cannot give it a foundation either. It leaves everything as it is" (*PI*, 124).

In this distrust of "progress," there is nothing of the enthusiasm of American pragmatism. It expresses, instead, a more characteristically European attitude, amounting to the belief that the longstanding practices of humankind embody a wisdom that is not likely to be matched by current fads and that should not be assailed by skeptical doubts. Our "forms of life" are fine when seen in the right light. Our objections to them are hollow and derive from illusory demands. Contingency presents no problem so long as philosophers refrain from inventing or at least elaborating standards that make our values and practices look bad.

This respect for our "workaday opinions" is one of the surprising similarities between Santayana and Wittgenstein. Santayana announces as early as the preface to *Scepticism and Animal Faith* his belief that "the shrewd orthodoxy" of humankind is in the end more nearly right than any of the special schools of philosophy. The entire edifice of animal faith he constructs is meant to be the articulation of the beliefs we tacitly embrace when we engage in the activities of life.

There is a further remarkable resemblance between Santayana and Wittgenstein. Both identify traditional philosophy as the source of the problems we have with contingency, and both attack it for advocating inapt, unreasonable, illusory, or absurd criteria of justification. Skepticism is inescapable, Santayana points out, so long as certainty is the aim and ultimate standard of knowledge. Seeking absolute assurance or transcendent grounding isolates philosophy from the concerns of life and empties it of all content: we are left gaping in silence at the immediacies of the moment.

Such reduction to solipsism of the present moment, however, has two marvelously positive consequences. The first is recognition that an honest philosophy demands standards different from absolute certainty. Successful animal life defines the criteria to which we must adhere if we are to retain a connection between what we think and what we unhesitatingly do. This is the grounding insight of the philosophy of animal faith Santayana proceeds to detail, of the system of ideas designed to capture the beliefs every animal's activities confirm. This system does not shrink from accepting contingency, uncertainty, and the less than absolute status of all our practices. On this level, Santayana thinks philosophy must remain docile with respect to our habits of action or what we do as animals operating in a natural environment.

The second positive outcome of the skeptical reduction is the discovery of essence. It is ironic that someone who makes essence the centerpiece of his philosophy should claim not to be an essentialist. But, of course, Santayana is correct in this claim: the infinity of the realm of essence strips forms of their moral, epistemic, and metaphysical prerogatives. Precisely because there are so many essences and they constitute a nonhierarchical democracy, we cannot claim that any of them exhausts the nature of one or a group of existing things.

The realm of essence, in turn, makes the spiritual life possible. Here is the promise of transcendence for which philosophers have always looked, a way of escaping the crushing vicissitudes of animal life. But the transcendence is also ironic: while the flux touches the eternal at the top of every wave, the peace of essence cannot suffuse animal life. Pure intuition presents a frozen landscape, a frozen cosmos-scape, even a frozen infinity of possible disorders that yield no escape from contingency and no security.

Santayana's ironic transcendence of the flux is matched by his ironic acceptance of the legitimacy of human practices within it. From the perspective of each, the other is present only at the point of disappearance or insignificance. For the engaged animal, spirituality is a useless luxury. Considering the infinity of essence, however, the values of animal life constitute only an irrelevant local incident.

In one sense, the acceptance and the transcendence cancel out each other's claims to absoluteness, leaving a tragic sense of life or at least a pervasive sadness at the fleeting beauty that surrounds us.

The distinctively Santayanan response to contingency is shaped by the interplay between transcendence through the spiritual life and the situatedness of the animal. Having once intuited essences for their own sake, one can never take the values, projects, and practices of animal life with ultimate seriousness. At the same time, however, the attitude of detachment this generates is easily combined with respect, shared by Wittgenstein, for the practical wisdom of the active animal. In one aspect, therefore, Santayana's response to contingency also reminds us of the Stoics. If contingency rules the world, we must face it bravely as one of the ultimate facts. But that need not keep us from participating in whatever even vaguely sensible practices may flourish in our society, for in the long run and from a cosmic standpoint, all of it matters not at all.

The discussion of contingency cannot be exhaustive within the limited scope of this book. Yet, in the current philosophical climate, it would be considered seriously lacking if it failed to make mention of the ideas of Richard Rorty. The notion of contingency plays a central role in his work, and, in extensive writings on the subject, he has developed his own view of how we might best respond to it.

Along with most other twentieth century philosophers, Rorty embraces contingency. Those who wish to deny or to escape it are perpetually inventing "final vocabularies."[13] The task of what he calls "ironists" is to think in such a way as to displace or discredit such final vocabularies. No way of thinking and speaking is ultimate or final in the sense that it cannot be resituated in a new context or replaced by a useful but different vocabulary. Rorty credits "strong poets" with the ability to imagine and initiate such plays or movements of language.[14]

Echoing a central theme of postmodernists, Rorty believes that irony is a powerful weapon against the absolutizing demands of traditional philosophy. It often succeeds in revealing the contingency below the surface of our languages, institutions, and practices. Yet Rorty is much more ready to endorse the value and legitimacy of Western liberal democracies than postmodern thinkers tend to be. Thus he wants to detach public lives and political solidarity from the private irony that sees the inevitable contingency of our practices and values.

He also wishes to distance functioning practices from the demands of foundationalist philosophy. He speaks of a "post-philosophical" culture and suggests that there is little or nothing for philosophers to do after critical detachment has been achieved. Broadly speaking, the institutions of Western civilization are in order as they are, and whatever changes might be necessary do not require the sort of thought that has characteristically been called "philosophical."

This suggests that Rorty offers a combination of the approaches to contingency we have already seen. He combines Dewey's contextualism with postmodern irony and Wittgenstein's conservative tendencies. Like all but one of the philosophers we have examined, he accepts the contingency of our fundamental practices, including our linguistic habits and vocabularies. Though he calls himself a pragmatist, he rejects, with postmodern thinkers, the reconstructive activism Dewey recommends. The source of this rejection, however, is not the suspicion that Dewey simply endorses the modernist or the Enlightenment project but Rorty's belief that we have already achieved a good solution to our political problems.[15]

This acceptance of the general outlines of liberalism bears an interesting family resemblance to Wittgenstein's conservatism and underlies Rorty's further agreement with Wittgenstein—a skeptical assessment of the role philosophy can play in public life. The philosophical task, for Rorty, exhausts itself in the continual struggle against final vocabularies. We are wise, he argues, to reinscribe or recontextualize such vocabularies so we can provide at least some protection from the totalizing and absolutizing tendencies of the modern age. The significant political task is that of enlarging the "we" of Western liberalism, but here again philosophy cannot contribute much.[16] We thus see that Rorty's response to contingency is not radically novel or original but consists of elements already present in the intellectual climate of our day.

There is yet another kinship between Rorty and Santayana that bears mention. Santayana's appropriation of contingency takes the form of a radical distinction between two sorts of consciousness. The first is the experience of the animal engaged in the business of living, the second the detached intensity of the spiritual life. In some ways, this distinction parallels the line Rorty draws between the public and the private. The spiritual life is a private affair in that it is impenetrable from the "outside," and the distinctions between act and object, and self and other, melt away in its eternity. It is clearly an alternative irreducible to the public life of the socially situated self.

From the perspective of such spirituality, the experience of the busy animal in us appears provincial. In the spiritual life, we explore the infinite reaches of the realm of essence. The contrast between this immensity and our minute strivings serves as a permanent source of irony. Although he offers no ontology to rival that of Santayana, Rorty has a corresponding source of ironic detachment: the strong poet provides an escape from the public world by sketching perspectives from which its care and problems fall away.

The similarities between Santayana and Rorty are easy to overstate. To balance the books, we need to call attention to at least one important subject concerning which they disagree. Both choose to characterize the private domain in aesthetic terms, but they view our relation to these realms differently. According to Santayana the pure intuition of essence—a sort of contemplation—is available for anyone at any time. For Rorty, by contrast, poetic redescription is an activity possible only in a context and against the background of prior descriptions.

Perhaps it is not surprising that both Rorty and Santayana have been attacked for introducing such a radical division into the midst of life. Such critics as John Stuhr and Simon Critchley charge that absorption in a private world may loosen the public bonds of social life.[17] They see both the spiritual life and private irony as escapist. And from the standpoint of the engaged life they are just that. But, both Santayana and Rorty would quickly remind us, we must be careful not to think that perspective privileged or final. In any case, at least Santayana knows that the heat of animal life soon brings us back to the affairs of the day.

Although we have not exhausted all the possible, or even all the interesting, responses to contingency, our discussion has shown at least some of the richness of the landscape. Evaluating such major philosophical approaches as pragmatism and postmodern thought requires that we locate them within just such a rich field of relevant alternatives. The work of Santayana and that of Wittgenstein add significantly to the profusion of alternatives. Consideration of them is, therefore, doubly valuable. Beyond their intrinsic importance and interest, they also help us see currently more popular responses to contingency in proper intellectual context.

Chapter 2

DISPLACING SKEPTICISM

Wittgenstein's treatment of the problems surrounding knowledge and certainty provide us with a clear example of the central theme of this book—thinking in the ruins. We have suggested that both Wittgenstein and Santayana reject the idea that knowledge and value require foundations. This can be no clearer than in *On Certainty*[1] where Wittgenstein is at pains to rethink and reevaluate the Cartesian tradition with its project of uncovering or establishing the foundations of human knowledge in a necessary first principle. In order to accomplish such a rethinking, Wittgenstein says, "Here once more there is needed a step like the one taken in relativity theory" (305).

What does he mean? If one supposes that space is absolute, there will be such a notion as absolute location, that is, location in space in relation to the absolute axis. Given such a view, one might take a number of different positions. One might be Cartesian in the sense of believing that there is such absolute location and that we can know the location of objects in relation to an absolute axis. Of course, such a standard must be carefully distinguished from everyday practical criteria by which we can locate objects but only relative to others. This will suffice for practical affairs, but it does not even approach "real location," which can be discovered only by the application of a sort of philosophical method. Mere relative location must ultimately be grounded in real location if we are really to know where anything is. Here we have an account that parallels the Cartesian distinction between practical beliefs and knowledge by means of clear and distinct ideas.[2]

15

Of course one might approach this same situation with skepticism of a Humean sort.[3] That is, one might grant that absolute location is the standard but believe that unfortunately we never know where we are by that standard. The skeptic here accepts the absolutist's standard of location—absolute location—but finds that given such a standard we can never know where anything is. Thus the notion of absolute location can be seen to underlie the views of both those who think they have achieved absolute certainty and those who think it is not to be found.

Into such an intellectual context enter Einstein and the theory of relativity. Location just is location relative to other things. The very ideas of absolute space and, with it, of absolute location are without useful employment. To know an object's location is always a matter of relative placement. Nashville is north of Miami and south of Chicago. The problem of absolute location, along with skepticism, falls away not by the discovery of an absolute axis firmly set in space but by a reorientation of our thinking about the problem. To put matters in Wittgensteinian terms, the problem is not solved but dissolved by showing how it rested on a mistaken picture.[4]

There are two extremely interesting and important passages which occur early in On Certainty that indicate that Wittgenstein has the Cartesian view clearly in focus. He says,

> The statement "I know that here is a hand" may then be continued: "for it is *my* hand that I'm looking at." Then a reasonable man will not doubt that I know.—Nor will the idealist [skeptic]; rather he will say that he was not dealing with the practical doubt which is being dismissed, but there is a further doubt behind that one.—That this is an *illusion* has to be shown in a different way (19).

In what is a clear parallel to the space example, Wittgenstein considers a distinction between practical doubt and another doubt which lies behind it. The latter is philosophical, or methodological, "doubt." That there is such a doubt is a function of the Cartesian picture of knowledge and that is said to be an illusion.

In another clear reference to the picture we are examining, Wittgenstein says, "Forget this transcendent certainty, which is connected with your concept of spirit" (*OC*, 47). Perhaps if we were Cartesian spirits—minds only accidentally connected to bodies—we might be able to operate with an absolute standard.[5] Nothing would turn on our acceptance or rejection of beliefs which are after all mere "adjustments of the mind anyway" (*OC*, 89). It is such a Cartesian theory of mind that allows for a conception of the human in terms of what may be called "the primacy of the epistemological." If, on the deepest level, we are minds with attached bodies, then the states of mind—doubt, knowledge, and certainty as Descartes conceives them—are the fundamental modes of reality. And this is exactly what Wittgenstein rejects in order to show that the supposed doubt behind "practical" doubt is an illusion. How does he do that?

We suggest that he does it by showing that the ways we actually use such terms as "know," "believe," and "evidence" have no similarity to their supposed foundational employment and that hence the epistemologist has no right to the terms in question. The first of these tasks is descriptive: we must be reminded of how we actually use language. That by itself, however, will not suffice. We must also be reminded of the larger context in which we use language. Here Wittgenstein's references to our "form of life" and its animal character become relevant.

Wittgenstein's strategy, then, is to block opening up the question of knowledge in the way that the skeptic wants.[6] He does this by denying the skeptic the language needed to frame the question. Skepticism thus becomes unintelligible because the key terms involved cannot be assigned relevant meaning. In trying to do philosophy in this way, that is, in the attempt to establish the skeptical, epistemic language-game, we tend to forget all that is necessary to make sense of claims to know or to doubt. "If you tried to doubt everything you would not get as far as doubting anything. The game of doubting itself presupposes certainty" (*OC*, 115).

Even here, there is room for misunderstanding. The epistemologist may agree but treat the presupposed certainty as an "epistemic posit" required to "play the game." But Wittgenstein rejects this, calling it "transcendent" and hence inaccessible certainty (*OC*, 47)—a merely "constructed point" (*OC*, 56)—that plays no role in our linguistic activities. The certainty presupposed by the "game of doubting" is not "akin to hastiness or superficiality, but . . . [is] a form of life. . . . But that means I want to conceive it as something that lies beyond being justified or unjustified; as it were, as something animal" (*OC*, 358–59).[7] What is at stake here lies outside the possibility of characterizing it in epistemic terms. Thus Wittgenstein talks about what "stands fast," "what gets its meaning from our proceedings," "an inherited background," "ungrounded ways of acting," and "facts fused into the foundations of our language-game," all of which are meant to focus our attention on a horizon within which epistemic terms have sense but which, at the same time, set limits to that sense (*OC*, 151, 229, 94, 110, 558). There are at least two very different forms of certainty. One is a certainty we arrive at through some considerations—a certainty that settles a doubt. But that certainty itself presupposes a deeper, de facto certainty given in and through our place in our environment.

What is the character of this second certainty? In various passages, Wittgenstein calls our attention to the priority of action for a proper understanding of the context of knowledge claims. He says, "Children do not learn that books exist, that armchairs exist, etc. etc.,—they learn to fetch books, sit in armchairs, etc. etc." (*OC*, 476). Here we see that our original relation to the things and activities around us is not one of epistemic assessment. Children do not learn that this or that is the case. Instead they engage in activities that involve things. They play with balls and sit in chairs. They build sandcastles and then knock them down. There is no question of knowledge here, and that is not because the truth is obvious. Rather it is because there is not yet room for such questions. As Wittgenstein goes on to say, "Later, questions about the existence of things do of course arise. 'Is there such a thing as a unicorn?' and so on. But such a question is possible only because as a rule no corresponding question presents itself" (*OC*, 476).

Questions of doubt and knowledge can arise only in the context created by our fundamental, active relations. Questions of truth and falsity, knowledge and doubt occur within what Wittgenstein calls "a picture of the world," but he also states that "I did not get my picture of the world by satisfying myself of its correctness nor do I have it because I am satisfied of its correctness. No: it is an inherited background against which I distinguish between true and false. The propositions describing this world-picture might be part of a kind of mythology" (OC, 94–95). Our "picture of the world" is not a matter of justified true beliefs. The picture constitutes the context in which such beliefs can arise. And when we reach this level, Wittgenstein says, "The difficulty is in realizing the groundlessness of our believing" (OC, 166).

The whole structure of belief is groundless precisely because it is the context within which grounding of individual beliefs can take place. But this ungroundedness is not a matter of propositions which lack foundations, but rather "it is an ungrounded way of acting" (OC, 110). The full character of Wittgenstein's view becomes clear in the following passage:

> I want to regard man here as an animal; as a primitive being to which one grants instinct but not ratiocination. As a creature in a primitive state. Any logic good enough for a primitive means of communication needs no apology from us. Language did not emerge from some kind of ratiocination (OC, 475).

Again:

> Now I would like to regard this certainty, not as something akin to hastiness or superficiality, but as a form of life. . . . But that means I want to conceive it as something that lies beyond being justified or unjustified; as it were, as something animal (OC, 358–59).

If language did not emerge out of ratiocination but out of animal instinct, then the fundamental character of certainty is that of the engaged animal for whom the environment is a field of action, not an occasion for puzzlement. Wittgenstein asks, "Does a child believe that milk exists? Or does it know that milk exists? Does a cat know that a mouse exists?" (OC, 478). The infant drinks the milk, and the cat chases the mouse. For neither of them is the object an epistemological posit. Only in contexts of activity can sensible epistemic questions arise.

As the discussion of *On Certainty* opens, Wittgenstein considers G. E. Moore's famous attempt to engage the skeptic at bedrock by claiming that he knows there is a hand before him.[8] Wittgenstein thinks this attempt to engage the skeptic fails because it accepts the fundamental presupposition of skepticism, namely the primacy of the epistemological. This view can be expressed in various ways. One form it takes is the following: "one thinks that the words 'I know . . .' are always in place where there is no doubt, and hence even where the expression of doubt would be unintelligible" (OC, 10). On this view, all our relations to the world are grounded in or derived from our epistemological relations. We have already seen that Wittgenstein's focus on action is tantamount to rejecting this. He argues, in addition, that such a view involves a misuse of the concept of knowledge. In subscribing to the primacy of the epistemological, "We just do not see how very specialized the use of 'I know' is" (OC, 11). Consider an example: "I know that a sick man is lying here? Nonsense! I am sitting at this bedside, I am looking attentively into his face.—So I don't know then, that there is a sick man lying here? Neither the question nor the assertion makes sense" (OC, 10). We might be said to know, in this situation, the nature of his illness or its seriousness or that his sister will be visiting in a short while, but it makes no sense to say that we know there is a sick man lying here.

There is something important to learn from the movement of thought exhibited in this passage. Notice that as soon as Wittgenstein denies that he knows something, the natural response is "So I don't know it then?" Or one might say, "Well, now that you mention it I certainly do know. . . ." In short the epistemic issue seems to have been broached. Either you know it or you do not, and the issue arises because Wittgenstein has singled out a feature of the situation for attention. His attempt to reject the epistemic language-game is taken as a move in the game. His focus on a particular element of the situation tends to lead us naturally to see epistemic relations just below the surface—there must be knowledge wherever there is no doubt!

This is a problem that arises when we try to talk or write philosophically about such cases, and it makes it almost impossible to set matters straight. When we talk or write about aspects of our situation to which we do not stand in an epistemic relation, we have shifted the context so that our normal relation to such things as the computer or the sidewalk has been interrupted. That is, as soon as we write that we do not know or just believe that the sidewalk is there, we focus epistemic attention on that very facet of the environment. Once the matter gets raised—once we single something out for attention—it seems appropriate to respond with a claim to know designed to overcome the doubt implied by the move to focus epistemic attention on it.

We raise questions about knowing or not knowing just when something is in doubt. If someone were to ask, by telephone perhaps, "Is there really a sick man in the room?" I might reply, "What do you mean? I am sitting right beside him," or "Of course, he is really sick. The doctor just examined him." The normal point of focusing epistemic attention on something is to resolve some problem connected with it. For example, the questioner may not have realized that I am right there in the room or that the doctor has already been in. What makes such questioning legitimate, of course, is that it occurs in a concrete context. Philosophical questions are, by contrast, not situated within the practices of daily life, so it is not clear what is at stake in asking and answering them.

G. E. Moore's famous comment about knowing that there is a hand before him would be at home just where there is a question or problem—some particular doubt that a questioner might have.[9] The very particularity of the contexts in which such doubts occur makes Moore's attempt to draw general philosophical conclusions misfire. Without such context, it is not clear what he means, that is, in what language-game his comment belongs. What is the particular doubt that Moore's assurance can be taken to set aside? There is none. On the other hand, as a reply to the skeptic, his comment is irrelevant because once the skeptic's question is raised, a sincere report that one knows cannot be an adequate answer. "For when Moore says 'I know that that's . . .' I want to reply 'you don't know anything!'—and yet I would not say that to anyone who was speaking without philosophical intention" (OC, 407).

What needs to be set aside is not a particular doubt for, after all, what Moore claims to know is just what "we all seem to know the same as he" (OC, 84). We need instead to rid ourselves of the "illusion" that epistemic terms are always appropriate and can correctly characterize our interactions with the world. As we have already seen, Moore is committed to that illusion just as much as the skeptic is and so cannot effectively show us that it is an illusion.[10]

But why should we think that it is an illusion? Is Descartes not entitled to his distinction between practical doubt and methodological doubt? And is not this all that is needed to get the epistemic language-game going? Of course, skeptics are not interested in the doubts that may or may not plague us in our daily affairs, but that does not imply that they have failed to identify some real doubts. It may make no sense to say "I know" in such situations, yet it is clearly true that I do. As Wittgenstein puts it,

> "Haven't I gone wrong and isn't Moore perfectly right? Haven't I made the elementary mistake of confusing one's thoughts with one's knowledge? Of course, I do not think to myself "The earth already existed for some time before my birth," but do I know it any the less?" (OC, 397).

After all, the inappropriateness of saying such things is merely a matter of the pragmatic conventions that govern our linguistic usage.[11] Just because we do not usually say the obvious, we are liable to mislead when we do, even if what we say is, looked at abstractly, quite true.

Philosophers want to distinguish between our everyday ways of speaking, which are under the rule of practical constraints, and what we would say on reflection. But in what would such reflection consist? Certainly not in adducing ordinary considerations, for they have already been dismissed as irrelevant. Would they be "philosophical" or "epistemological" considerations? Then this is just another version of the idea that behind practical doubt there lies a further sort of doubt which is theoretical or epistemological, or that behind our actual language there is another which is somehow free of the pitfalls of the first and in which we can gain a transcendent view of our activities.

The Wittgenstein of the *Tractatus* may have accepted such a possibility, but the Wittgenstein of the *Philosophical Investigations* clearly rejects it.[12] He says, "When philosophers use a word—'knowledge,' 'being,' 'object,' 'I,' 'proposition,' 'name'—and try to grasp the essence of the thing, one must always ask oneself: is the word ever actually used in this way in the language-game which is its original home?—What we do is to bring words back from their metaphysical to their everyday use" (117). Wittgenstein is not rejecting the legitimacy of technical language here, nor is he according some unjustified privileged status to ordinary use. The point is that if the epistemologist has a coherent language-game, that game has nothing to do with doubt or certainty. The conjuring trick has already been performed in the act of distinguishing mere practical doubt from methodological doubt. What criterion justifies the use of the term "doubt" in the latter phrase? Certainly not the standard that governs everyday use of "doubt," for we have already admitted that philosophical doubt is not an ordinary sort of uncertainty. But how can it be doubt at all if it bears little or no relation to our actual uses of the term "doubt"? And the force of Wittgenstein's descriptions of actual use demonstrates that it does not. So the skeptic's use of the term "doubt" bears as little relation to doubt as the chess master's use of the term "bishop" does to church hierarchy.

Epistemologists claim to be talking not about the everyday sorts of doubt, belief, and certainty, but about their specialized philosophical forms. What right do they have to the use of the corresponding terms at all? Wittgenstein describes how philosophers might think about it:

> One would like to say: "Everything speaks for, and nothing against the earth's having existed long before. . . ." Yet might I not believe the contrary after all? But the question is:

What would the practical effects of this belief be?—Perhaps someone says: "That's not the point. A belief is what it is whether it has any practical effects or not." One thinks: "It is the same adjustment of the human mind anyway" (OC, 89).

Here we have a typically philosophical use of the term "believe," employed abstractly and out of context. What reason is there to suppose that when we take away the practical effects and living context of believing, anything like belief is left over? Is belief merely a private, detached "adjustment of the human mind?" And what, after all, is that?[13] Whatever the epistemologist may have in mind must be connected with doubt and belief in some concrete way. "Or are we to say that *certainty* is merely a constructed point to which some things approximate more, some less closely? No. Doubt gradually loses its sense. This language-game just *is* like that" (OC, 56). Whatever the epistemologist is trying to say has nothing to do with certainty and doubt in any sense we can understand. The ideas that certainty is "a constructed point" and that belief is an "adjustment of the human mind" involve either a misuse of our language or the introduction of something that masquerades as a language but is in fact only an uninterpreted calculus. Our language is misused because "doubt gradually loses its sense." Alternatively, if epistemologists insist on the "integrity" of their use, their terms function as mere markers moved around in a game that has nothing to do with the language-game of doubt and certainty.[14]

The skeptic's uses of such terms as "doubt" and "certainty" are illicit in so far as they are confused with ordinary ones. Of course, skeptics may reply that there is no such confusion. In fact, they are at great pains to distinguish between mere ordinary doubt and the deeper doubt to which they wish to give voice. But this distinction is empty, for they have no basis for calling whatever philosophical ideas they might have in mind "doubt" and "certainty" in the first place. "Do you know or do you only believe that what you are writing down now are German [English] words? Do you only believe that 'believe' has this meaning? What meaning?" (OC, 486). Whatever we may be talking about, it is certainly not knowledge, belief, or doubt.

Here we see one way in which Wittgenstein's "descriptive method" interrupts skeptical thinking. When he describes actual uses of terms in relation to the skeptic's, the latter come to be seen as problematic and in need of justification. Why should we suppose that the skeptic is talking about *knowledge* or *belief* in the first place? We do not know what skeptics are saying because their key terms are given no meaning. We mistakenly suppose we know what "doubt" means, and we think that the term will retain its meaning even when it no longer functions in the ways with which we are familiar—"as if the sense were an atmosphere accompanying the word, which it carried with it into every kind of application" (*PI,* 117).

Skeptics can offer us only alternative uses of words—another language-game perhaps. They cannot expose the substructure of meaning, that is, analyze the ordinary sense of ordinary speech. As Wittgenstein says in *Philosophical Investigations,* "In what sense do the symbols of this language-game [the everyday one] stand in need of analysis? How far is it even possible to replace this language-game by . . . [the skeptic's]?—It [the skeptic's] is just another language-game, even though it is related to . . . [the ordinary one]" (64). So, at best, the skeptic can be seen only as proposing that we deploy a different language-game, that we conduct our affairs differently. But is even this possible?

In *Philosophical Investigations* Wittgenstein tells us that to imagine a language-game means to imagine a form of life (19). He means by this that to imagine a language is not merely a matter of imagining how words interconnect with other words, but also a matter of seeing what role these interconnected sets of words play in the lives of those who use them. So, he says, "it is easy to imagine a language consisting only of orders and reports"—in battle, for example. But now skeptics are confronted with a real difficulty. How are we supposed to deploy their proposed new language-game? To what actions and practices should we imagine it connected? Of what form of life can we imagine it as a part?

It is easy enough to imagine the changes in our linguistic patterns that are recommended by the skeptic. Think, for example, of a person who always says

"I am sure" on occasions where (for example) there is sureness in the reports we make (in an experiment, for example, we look through a tube and report the color we see through it). If he does, our immediate inclination will be to check what he says. But if he proves to be perfectly reliable, one will say that his way of talking is merely a bit perverse, and does not affect the issue. One might for example suppose that he had read sceptical philosophers, become convinced that one can know nothing, and that is why he has adopted this way of speaking. Once we are used to it, it does not infect practice (OC, 524).

But then his "doubt" or "sureness" concerns only what we should *say* on various occasions and doubt that exhibits itself only in conversation is not real doubt,[15] it cannot make out its claim to be doubt at all.

Is there a coherent form of life—a pattern of human practices—of which the skeptic's language-game can be an ingredient? The very terms of the question rule out a positive answer since they involve patterns of action and other human beings, realities the skeptic does not accept. Skeptics from Hume to Santayana have seen that, in the end, philosophical skepticism is inconsistent with action.[16] The very point of philosophical skepticism, global or limited, is to undermine whole classes of claims and to refuse to distinguish acceptable from unacceptable discourses. Thus skeptics tend to recommend that we live with the crowd even as we maintain our epistemic purity. But what, after all, is "epistemic purity" and what does it have to do with knowledge and doubt? We cannot maintain that there is a deeper doubt behind our ordinary doubts unless we can articulate a form of life in which the skeptic's language-game can be at home. If Wittgenstein, Santayana, and others are correct, this cannot be done.[17] And that means that we cannot imagine the full-bodied practice or language-game of skepticism. Skepticism is but a game played with words.

Santayana finds skepticism just as wanting as does Wittgenstein, and for closely related reasons. His attack on skepticism focuses not on the language used to express skeptical doubts, but on the criterion by which the skeptic convicts all putative knowledge of inadequacy. His strategy is to permit all skeptical questions and thereby show that a rigorous skepticism, though in its own terms irrefutable, reduces itself to silence. Interestingly, though Wittgenstein's strategy is not to let skeptics have the key notions needed for asking their withering questions, he agrees that once their moves are made, their position becomes irrefutable. So while one rejects the starting point of wholesale doubt and the other pushes the program to self-destruction, both thinkers concur that skepticism cannot be defeated on its own ground and fails in the end only because it is incompatible with action or the practices that constitute our lives.

Santayana begins *Scepticism and Animal Faith* with the commitment to give skeptics the benefit of doubting everything they can. He views Descartes's efforts at doubt halfhearted: it is not difficult to question, for example, the idea that wherever there is a thought, there must be a thinker. Instead he wants to be steadfast and question everything: "Let me then push scepticism as far as I logically can, and endeavor to clear my mind of illusion, even at the price of intellectual suicide" (*SAF*, p. 10).

He perseveres in skeptical questioning until he reaches bedrock in solipsism of the present moment, a position revealing that epistemic suicide, or at least bankruptcy, is indeed the outcome of a rigorous program of doubt.

The strategy of the questioning is to detach beliefs from what is palpably before us. The present is immune to doubt; in our beliefs we embellish on what is directly noted by interpreting it or relating it to things beyond our ken. To find the element of the given in a flapping flag, for example, we must bracket everything we know about it. That it is the flag of the United States, that the wind is making it move, and that it flutters over a post office are only opinions that may well be false. Even the conviction that it is a flag takes the mind beyond the immediate to tacit comparisons with other bits of suspended, pendulous material. And the thought that it is fluttering involves such implicit beliefs that it is not motionless and that at least a part of it is unattached to something rigid.

This may misleadingly suggest that in separating out the given, Santayana wants to eliminate all conceptual materials. But his aim is not to rest in sensory immediacy. This would take him in the direction of the sense-datum analyses popular in the 1930s, with all their attendant difficulties. He is closer in spirit to Husserl's bracketing, in which the entirety of the phenomenon is retained in consciousness, with all reference to existence eliminated. Santayana's interest thus is not in the sensory residue of perceptual life but in what is left over, sensory or conceptual, if we refuse to believe anything. So, in the case of the flag, the immediacy may be a single exquisitely sensuous and inexpressible flutter, or it may be the entire vision of flag-flapping-over-post-office, so long as it is taken as a *vision*, that is, as an unconnected theme that signifies nothing. The key is to believe nothing about how what is present may be related to anything else, but to stare wide-eyed at the scene. Even our current beliefs may be parts of the scene, so long as we merely note them as opinions without embracing them.

In attempting to detach belief from the immediacy of conscious life, Santayana draws on both an intellectual and a moral tradition. The former strikes a blow for epistemic purity by eliminating suppositions and reducing all things to what a cold eye perceives them to be. Hume's analyses of the scanty sensory basis of our cherished beliefs in self and God fall in this category. The latter grows out of the cosmic suspicion of life associated with Indian thought, but accessible to anyone in moments of great stress or stunned unreality in the early morning. The moral edge of the suspicion is not to let oneself be deceived about what ultimately matters: the show of shadows that we call the world surely does not. Ultimate skeptics are people who observe all the hints and innuendos of the world and believe none of them. They view the immediate out of relation to everything else. It is self-identically itself, and, for all we know, it may be all there is.

The separation of fact from fancy, of what is directly given from opinion, presupposes a criterion of knowledge. The standard this sets is very high: it is the certainty of presence. Contrary to what has been supposed,[18] the criterion is not discursive, relating to propositions and demanding of them that their denial be self-contradictory. Such a rationalist standard aims at certainty no less than the one Santayana's skeptic embraces. But it is curiously distant and questionable as a standard precisely because it sets requirements for *propositions*. Relating in thought the elements of which propositions consist takes time, so the arguments against the veracity of memory count also against our ability to articulate meaningful judgments. For this reason, propositions as units of discursive thought fall early in the skeptical campaign. Setting a standard for them would collapse the cognitive quest too soon: the first doubt of memory would leave us with nothing that could either meet the criterion or fail by it.

The criterion on the basis of which Santayana decides what may be doubted and what may not is that of presence. This demands certainty no less than the rationalist discursive standard. It measures assurance, however, not by the contradictoriness or inconceivability of the denial of what we think, but by intuitive possession. It declares that anything not immediately before the mind is at risk, that we can trust only what we see. Such seeing is, of course, not something we do with the eyes, whose existence as physical organs is a matter only of belief. "Seeing" is, rather, a metaphor for awareness, for what appears in the light of consciousness when that is viewed as "the total *inner* difference between being awake or asleep" (*RB*, p. 572).

The criterion of presence or intuitive possession calls for a focus on the immediate. Accordingly, Santayana says, "I shall prove no sceptic if I do not immediately transfer all my trust from the existence reported to the appearance reporting it" (*SAF*, p. 43). What we call "appearance" in our philosophical reflections is, of course, not judged or experienced as appearance by skeptics. Absorbed in the immediate object, they are unmindful of anything beyond. There is, for them, no reality other than what spreads out as the object of consciousness; anything past that small given world is conjectural, with our access to it restricted to feeble beliefs.

Moreover, although from an external standpoint we may speak of the immediate as an object of consciousness, skeptics must deny themselves any such luxury. The distinction between subject and object is not internal to what appears. The subject or mind, or what

Santayana calls the act of intuition, is not among the constituents of the given. We may infer that the panorama before us is part of a larger world or that, at the very least, it occurs at some time for awhile. But these are speculations only and a steadfast skeptic must disregard them as questionable. That the scene we enjoy is an object appearing to a subject is likewise open to doubt: nothing in it testifies to the further existence of an observer, and even if something did, it could form the basis only of a tenuous illation.

Only the immediately present answers, then, the demand for intuitive possession and it is "a surface form, without roots, without origin or environment, without a seat or a locus" (*SAF*, p. 22). This form carries no meaning: it neither expresses nor refers to any ulterior facts. Since existence is to be deployed in a changing environment, the immediate scene cannot even be said to exist. Santayana announces that nothing given exists[19] and nothing existent is ever given. What is present fills out reality. As a changeless, though perhaps momentary, totality with no external relations, it does not reside in a larger world but constitutes the only one there is.

When Santayana declares that "Existence, then, not being included in any immediate datum, is a fact always open to doubt" (*SAF*, p. 39–40), he announces a skepticism without limits. It can be defeated only by our being certain of what is directly present. Yet we can assert nothing about the constitution, relations, and environment of this datum. Because judging is a synthesis of elements taking time, we can form no propositions about it, cannot even assert its self-identity. We can thus find certainty only at the cost of intellectual life. We can stare at the datum with open eyes, but the look is vacant. We can feel assured in our possession of what appears, but such certainty yields no knowledge. We cannot be wrong in what we plainly see, yet the sense of assurance is hollow. We know nothing about the datum; we simply hold it in an uncomprehending gaze. So long as we want significance or knowledge on the basis of the criterion of presence, the skeptic always wins.

The victory of skepticism, achieved on its own terms, is at once its undoing. There is an air of unreality about the entire enterprise: the intellectual foundations of everything seem to come tumbling down, yet none of our practices is in the least affected. The persistent questioning leaves our workaday ideas and values untouched. Though we profess to doubt the existence of others, we happily converse with them. We say we cannot *know* that there is a refrigerator in the house, yet we find our way to it for a midnight snack.[20]

One way of characterizing this anomaly is by saying that philosophy has lost its honesty. Honest thinkers stand in philosophy exactly where they stand in daily life.[21] Skeptics violate this requirement by feigning uncertainty, pretending that we cannot be sure about the very things we take for granted in our practices. Theirs is not a sincere hesitation or disbelief but an intellectual game, a game of words, without concrete purpose or results. They show little interest in real outcomes: what matters is how well the moves are made, the thrust and parry of abstract argument. The ceaseless questioning becomes, in this way, an amusement of philosophers, a way in which they test their mental agility.

The gulf it opens between thought and action, between theory and practice, marks the irrelevance of skepticism and justifies bypassing it. There are, of course, legitimate practical doubts in daily life, the generalization of which begets the skeptical enterprise. One may doubt, for example, that one has enough money to pay one's bills this month. Such concerns, as Peirce liked to point out,[22] are the legitimate starting points of inquiry and action: not being sure about the balance of one's bills and earnings, one may proceed to add them up and then to take steps to reduce the first or to increase the second. The generalization of the concern, however, is inappropriate. Even if there is reason for misgivings about one's finances, it does not make sense to question the bank's readiness to honor one's checks to the limit of one's account, the willingness of others to accept payment denominated in dollars, or the general fact that payments decrease rather than add to what one owes.[23]

The contexts of everyday existence justify specific and limited doubts. But no practices demand or even permit suspecting everything. Wholesale skepticism can gain plausibility only by operating at a remove from what we do and by employing what seems a temptingly tough but is an unrealistically high standard of knowledge.

Intuitive possession of the object of knowledge is neither necessary nor possible in ordinary life. Animals often disappointed in their search might think that it would be wonderful never to be wrong. The contingencies of life and our finitude as cognitive agents prevent this wish from ever coming true. To demand it nevertheless is to foist an alien and irrelevant ideal on the customs and habits that serve us well enough. Instead of such outlandish standards, we need to let the contexts and purposes of our inquiries set the criteria by which we judge their success.

Santayana and Wittgenstein are in remarkable agreement in their assessment of skepticism. Both think that persistent and unallayable doubt shows that something has gone wrong in the intellectual enterprise, and both blame philosophers for the distortion. Neither believes that skepticism can be defeated on its own terms, but they maintain that those terms are irrelevant to the actual processes of inquiry. They are at one on the strategy of combating skepticism: both reject absolute certainty as the standard of cognition and want to return the criteria of knowledge to the looser practices of ordinary life. Although Wittgenstein thinks of these practices as language-games, he is keenly aware that they involve much more than an exchange of words. They are forms of cooperative endeavor in which language functions in a context of natural objects and human actions. Even as primitive a language-game as builders asking for and handing each other blocks shows the rich natural setting of such communication.[24] What counts as knowledge can be determined only with reference to specific language-games, and these games constitute the manner in which we lead our lives.[25]

Santayana's ultimate stress is a little different from Wittgenstein's. Instead of focusing on the social element of communication, he concentrates on our lives as animals in a natural world.[26] Even in that context, however, the level of assurance needed for knowledge differs with circumstances, with what is at stake, and with our purposes. We require, for instance, much greater care in the diagnosis of HIV infection than in deciding whether rejecting a shot in basketball is a case of goaltending. So much hangs on a correct determination in the former case that we insist on the latest techniques and on double-checking the results. In the latter case, we think that a quick glance by the nearest referee is enough. Neither of the findings approximates certainty, but if they issue in beliefs that are justified by relevant criteria and that we can embody in appropriate actions, they are good enough.

There is one point on which Wittgenstein and Santayana part company. The performance of philosophy in the quest for knowledge and elsewhere gives Wittgenstein profound misgivings about its value and legitimacy. He sees little good coming from such intellectual enterprises. Accordingly he resists making generalizations about knowledge, its criterion, and its sources that might amount to even a tentative philosophical account. He is satisfied to unmask the decontextualized surreality of the skeptical reduction and to show that knowledge can be generated and assessed only in concretely situated language-games.

Santayana, on the other hand, retains a certain ironic attachment to philosophy. The embrace is ironic because, agreeing on this with the majority of post-Kantian thinkers, he has no expectation that systematic reflection can explore or reveal arcane reaches of existence. Yet he sees value in a clear general understanding of the nature of knowledge, of human striving, and of the good in order for us to get straight on "the chief issue, the relation of man and his spirit to the universe" (SAF, p. viii). He does not think that any account of the features of human experience can sensibly claim universal truth. But, though the validity of philosophical generalizations is limited by the nature of our organs and by our animal circumstances, they at least obviate "occasions for sophistry by giving to everyday beliefs a more accurate and circumspect form" (SAF, p. v).

Accordingly Santayana proceeds to develop a philosophy of "animal faith." Modestly, this system leaves it to our multiple practices to determine what constitutes knowledge in one or another area of life. To such plurality of standards it adds only a thin layer of generality by offering a criterion for the evaluation of philosophical claims. The standard is that of the honesty to which we referred earlier, requiring us to believe only what we can enact. Viewed as a method for generating philosophical ideas, the examination of animal faith becomes a search for the beliefs that are implicated in our ordinary actions. When hunger drives us to look for food, for example, we assume the independent existence of the objects of our pursuit. Similarly, when we jump out of the way of a car speeding toward us, we testify to our sincere belief that independently existing things enjoy significant causal powers.

The philosophy of animal faith is designed to be simply the systematic articulation of what all of us believe and hence act out in our practices, even if such commitments rarely rise to explicit consciousness. It constitutes the expression in the language of reflection of the "shrewd orthodoxy which the sentiment and practice of laymen maintain everywhere" (*SAF*, p. v). As a philosophy to counteract the intellectual depredations of skepticism, it claims no certainty. The context meant to situate and to justify it is the travail of human life throughout which we attempt to stabilize the contingencies of nature by means of complex cooperative practices.

In saying "If one tried to advance theses in philosophy, it would never be possible to debate them, because everyone would agree with them" (*PI*, 128), Wittgenstein clearly has something close to Santayana's "shrewd orthodoxy" in mind. Although he does not develop a specialized vocabulary to articulate the views of this orthodoxy, his position about the role and future of philosophy is closer to Santayana's than it might at first appear. For, much as he tries, Wittgenstein finds it difficult to avoid committing himself to some substantive philosophical views. And on the other side, even when he speaks of realms of being, Santayana presents his philosophy of animal faith as no more than a summary or clarification of common human beliefs. Nothing that strays far from the actual human practices of cognition and action has much credibility in their eyes. Both are refugees from skepticism who embrace what we do and celebrate it as needing no external justification.

Chapter 3

THE CONTINGENCY OF VALUES

As we saw with regard to the treatment of cognition, both Santayana and Wittgenstein hold that there can be no universal theory of knowledge in any strong sense of the term. They maintain, instead, that the criteria of knowledge emerge out of the multiplicity of practices in which we are immersed. The concrete content of knowledge claims cannot be evaluated by reference to the demands of universal reason for the simple reason that there is no such thing. Our thinking is situated within human practices and takes its shape, its purposes, and its criteria from them. Remarkably, to undermine the claims of universal reason is at once to eliminate the basis of skepticism, for the skeptical enterprise can get off the ground only by ignoring the situated character of all our claims to know.

In the light of their attitude to cognition, it would not be surprising to see Wittgenstein and Santayana offer resembling approaches to understanding morality. The truth, however, is that nowhere in his later writings does Wittgenstein deal systematically with the topic of values. He offers no account of what is valuable or of what the good life might be. There are hints in *Culture and Value,* and there are ways of reading *Philosophical Investigations* in light of the ethical parts of the *Tractatus* that are highly suggestive.[1] But, in the final analysis, Wittgenstein simply does not speak in detail to the philosophical problems that surround valuation. The silence is not accidental. It will become clear as we reconstruct the way he thinks about normativity that a neutral stance or distance from value commitment is in fact a necessary consequence of his view. For Wittgenstein the content of moral thinking is determined by the interplay among our practices, institutions, preferences, and ways of speaking, all of which are elements of our form of life.[2] Not only does Wittgenstein avoid substantive normative questions, he also devotes very little explicit thought to the status of ethical or value judgments. There are a few suggestive passages, but no sustained discussion of the sort that *On Certainty* presents on knowledge claims.

We will begin, therefore, with an examination of the status of ethical judgments from the perspective of Wittgenstein's reflections on meaning and language.[3] We will develop the general outlines of his view with constant reference to and by analogy with his treatment of knowledge. This largely constructive procedure will provide us with a clear picture of where Wittgenstein stands which in turn will serve as the basis of a systematic comparison with Santayana.

Wittgenstein excludes the possibility of a foundational approach to value claims. The content of such claims must be determined by our practices and philosophy plays no role in their justification. With value claims, as with knowledge claims, "What we do is to bring words back from their metaphysical to their everyday use" (*PI*, 116). With this motto, Wittgenstein announces his move away from a universalist philosophy and the return to situated human practices. The move puts to rest a number of traditional problems that have plagued ethical thinking.

At the center of Wittgenstein's later work is the rejection of the possibility of what has been called transcendence.[4] He came to believe that we cannot achieve the ultimate goal of the *Tractatus*—a view of the world as the totality of facts. Of course, he does not simply deny this possibility, for such a denial would invoke the very idea it rejects. Instead he displaces transcendence in a variety of ways throughout *Philosophical Investigations*. Sometimes he does this by calling attention to the radical gap between the philosopher's questions formulated in the light of the possibility of transcendence and the situated character of our actual practices. Nothing like the philosopher's concerns is at stake in coming to terms with our practices. The "trick" philosophers play is to misdirect our attention and so make it appear that their inquiries are somehow continuous with our everyday activities.[5] But as Wittgenstein points out in the first section of the *Philosophical Investigations* with regard to the philosopher's notion of meaning, "No such thing was in question here" (1). In just the way and for just the reasons Wittgenstein and Santayana reject a foundationalist approach to knowledge, they also distance themselves from the enterprise of attempting to provide foundations for our values. By rejecting transcendence, Wittgenstein at once abjures the idea that we can get behind or below our practices to ground them in some absolute structure or principle.

There is a key passage that deserves special attention. In 241 and 242 of *Philosophical Investigations* Wittgenstein comments,

> So you are saying that human agreement decides what is true and what is false?—It is what human beings *say* that is true and false; and they agree in the *language* they use. That is not agreement in opinion but in form of life.
>
> If language is to be a means of communication there must be agreement not only in definitions but also (queer as this may sound) in judgments. This seems to abolish logic, but does not do so.—It is one thing to describe methods of measurement, and another to obtain and state results of measurement. But what we call "measuring" is partly determined by a certain constancy in results of measurement.

Here Wittgenstein appears to be rejecting a crude form of relativism because it fails to take account of two different sorts of agreement— agreement in opinions and agreement in form of life. What is the difference he has in mind?

The second paragraph gives us the answer. There he presents us with a contrast between agreement in definitions and in judgments, with the latter corresponding to agreement in form of life. But are judgments not themselves simply opinions? And are we then not brought back to the claim that human agreement decides what is true and what is false? This may appear as a powerful objection, yet it misconceives the thrust of Wittgenstein's discussion. He is calling attention not to judgments as true or false opinions, but to the *fact* that by following certain procedures we achieve "a certain constancy in results." The important point is not the possibility of truth but the fact of agreement. If we were not the sort of creatures that get the same results following such procedures as placing a rod against an object and reading off a number, those procedures would not be measuring. That is, they would not play the role measuring does in our current activities. We might very well continue to go through the motions, but we would not be *measuring*. The sort of agreement we have here is not one that is the product of inquiry, discussion, or thought. Nor is it the sort of conventional agreement we achieve by stipulation. So it is not an agreement either in opinion or in definition. It is de facto similarity or alikeness.[6] Human beings just are similar in this particular way. We get the same results when we employ a particular method. More important perhaps, we are alike in being able to be taught to use the method and to use it reliably.

There is nothing arbitrary or conventional about this agreement, and there is nothing subjective about it. In a certain sense, of course, it is contingent; we might not have been alike in this or that particular way. But had we not been, nothing or something very different would count as measuring for us. And, it is worth noting, we could not describe that state of affairs the way we have just described things as they stand now, since key elements of that description, "measurement," for example, would not be available to us.

In part 2 of *Philosophical Investigations*, Wittgenstein says, "Does it make sense to say that people generally agree in their judgments of colour? What would it be like for them not to?—One man would say a flower was red which another called blue, and so on.—But what right should we have to call these people's words 'red' and 'blue' *our* 'colour-words'?" (226). The problem with the question here is that it invites us to think of two independent elements—judgments of color and agreement in the use of color terms. But the second is constitutive of the first. For the mark "blue" to be a color word, there must be general agreement in its use. Were there no such agreement, the mark in question and the others which, as things stand, are in the same family would not play the role they do for us; they would not be color words. We cannot separate the meanings of our words from the facts that surround their use.[7] To think that we can is to fail to grasp the difference between agreement in opinion and agreement in form of life.

Wittgenstein thus contends that being alike in certain ways—agreeing in form of life—is necessary for language to be a means of communication. And further, though this contention may seem to undercut or even abolish logic, in fact it does not do so, for it does not blur the distinction between "describing methods of measurement" (logic) and "obtaining and stating results of measurement" (empirical inquiry). Thus the normative character of logic is not compromised, even though it finds its ground in de facto similarities and depends on the fact that we agree in making certain judgments.

What does this imply about ethical judgments? What Wittgenstein says about cognitive matters applies to values as well. This does not mean that human agreement decides which ethical judgments are right and which are wrong; the important agreement concerns not what human beings say but the moral language they use, and the practice of using that language constitutes not agreement in opinion but in form of life.[8] If ethical language is to be a means of communication, there must be agreement not only in ethical definitions but also (queer as this may sound) in ethical judgments. It may appear that the need for such agreement in ethical judgments abolishes the idea of a "logic of moral language," but it does not.

Those who think it does are likely to point out that ethical language is essentially normative (as is logic), but it loses its normativity if it depends on nothing beyond the de facto sameness of particular judgments. Wittgenstein can respond by reminding the objector that he rejects the dichotomy on which such an argument depends. By rejecting transcendence as it appears in the *Tractatus*, he also disposes of the hermetic distinction between meaning and fact. Just as a particular procedure cannot count as measuring unless we actually get the same results when following it, so we cannot engage in common moral discussion unless we begin with some de facto similar judgments. If human beings did not agree in finding certain actions, events, and states of character abhorrent or satisfying, there would be no moral perspective. We could then offer no reasons to each other, and we could not engage in rational evaluation. If we were not alike in these ways, as we might well not be, nothing or something very different would count as ethical discourse for us.[9]

Note carefully, however, that if we were not alike in the relevant sorts of ways, we could not describe such a state of affairs as we just did. For key elements of that description ("reason," "evaluation," and "moral perspective," for example) would not be available to us. People who think that we would have these concepts, regardless, tacitly appeal to a decontextualized transcendence. This is what Wittgenstein's interlocutor seems to presuppose when he asks, "So you are saying that human agreement decides what is true and what is false." Wittgenstein's point is that we cannot stand outside of the practices within which and in terms of which our descriptions make sense.

Throughout *Philosophical Investigations,* Wittgenstein insists on the situated, embedded character of language. Our speaking takes place within a larger practice of conversation, and this has its place or places in other practices of building, caring, curing, measuring, and counting. Those practices and the human reactions and responses involved with them constitute our form or forms of life. There can be no thought of stripping away the social, conventional aspects of life to arrive at the "natural." That would be to try once more to ground language in something nonlinguistic. But Wittgenstein reminds us that "commanding, questioning, recounting, chatting, are as much a part of our natural history as walking, eating, drinking, playing" (*PI,* 25).

This is the sense in which we can best understand Wittgenstein's contention that "to imagine a language means to imagine a form of life" (*PI,* 19). Imagining a language is not simply a matter of imagining a syntactical structure—marks that flow together in some fashion governed by conventional rules. To imagine a language is to imagine those marks within a play of human abilities and activities. That is why "it is easy to imagine a language consisting only of orders and reports in battle" (*PI,* 19). After all, "speaking a language is part of an activity, or of a form of life" (*PI,* 23).

We need to be reminded of who we are and what role bits of language actually play in our lives. In this way we become reacquainted with certain "extremely general facts of nature" (*PI*, 36) in terms of which we can explain the significance of particular concepts. Wittgenstein says, "It often happens that we only become aware of the important *facts,* if we suppress the question 'why?'; and then in the course of our investigations these facts lead us to an answer" (*PI*, 471). When, in various contexts, Wittgenstein points to such "important facts," he is calling attention to our form of life and to the place of particular segments of language within it. So, in the final analysis, "What has to be accepted, the given, is—so one could say—forms of life" (*PI*, part 2, 226).

This reference to the given is designed to remind us of the traditional foundationalist project in epistemology and to reject it. Refusal to accept the validity of this cognitive enterprise is at once refusal to countenance its twin project in ethics. Speaking of forms of life directs us back to concrete human practices in which our activities are situated.

To understand what Wittgenstein has in mind, we must draw an important distinction. It would be easy to misread him by supposing that he espouses a sort of stoic acceptance of whatever exists. Nothing could be further from the truth. The recommendation to accept our form of life is not an invitation to moral inactivity. It is a culminating piece of philosophical, or perhaps antiphilosophical, advice. The world around us is full of moral problems that require serious attention and conscientious action. But such real-life moral problems are not addressed by philosophy conceived as an activity of problematizing our practices. Wittgenstein's reminders thrust us back into the midst of our practices, with all their complexity and with all the problems to which they give rise. These real problems, encompassing the full range of moral issues, require action and not the ineffectual analysis of philosophers.

Philosophy in the traditional sense has nothing to contribute to the solution of such problems, and Wittgenstein's therapy is designed to free us of the illusory demand for justifying the forms of life that frame them.[10] Still, there is something to be said for the idea that the objective of philosophy is ethical in a fundamental way. For it aims, even in the view of the later Wittgenstein, at an acceptance of the world or of our form of life in it. Such acceptance is, in a certain sense, the solution to the problem of wrongly supposing that we are in need of philosophical insight. That, however, is not the end of the matter, as it might have been thought to be by the author of the *Tractatus*. It is just the beginning of dealing with the problems of life.

We must stress the point that, for the later Wittgenstein, so-called philosophical problems are to be dissolved. He does not claim to find the solution to a single real problem of life. Rather his method allows him (and us) to turn attention away from illusory philosophical issues toward the problems involved in living.[11] By rejecting the terms necessary for its formulation, Wittgenstein frees us of such worn philosophical issues as "the meaning of life."

The traditional philosophical picture misconceives the nature of ethical reasons and judgments by attempting to grasp them as a totality from the outside. From this perspective, they can and must be justified only by a set of self-evident ethical principles or by some suitable nonethical ground. Without such justification, every ethical judgment seems to depend on some other, equally problematic ethical judgment, and the whole domain appears to lack the philosophical structure or closure thought essential.[12] The traditional view holds, therefore, that ethics must be constituted as a normatively neutral discourse or that it must be justified by reference to some absolute ground.

Wittgenstein thinks, however, that in terms of our actual ethical practices such a perspective is altogether irrelevant. This shines through clearly in some of his remarks recorded by G. E. Moore:

> What Aesthetics tries to do, he said, is to give *reasons*. . . . Reasons, he said in Aesthetics, are "of the nature of further descriptions," e.g., you can make a person see what Brahms was driving at by showing him lots of pieces by Brahms, or by comparing him to a contemporary author; and all that Aesthetics does is "to draw your attention to a thing," to "place things side by side." He said that if, by giving "reasons" of this sort, you make the other person "see what you see" but it "still doesn't appeal to him" that is "an end" of

the discussion . . . And he said that the same sort of "reasons" were given . . . in Ethics. (As quoted in *Ethics without Philosophy*, pp. 128–29)

We give reasons in ethics by redescribing what is questionable, so as to bring it into contact with what is not questionable or vice versa. Consider such statements as "Abortion is wrong because it is, after all, a matter of killing a child" and "One should not eat meat because animals have feelings." Such reason giving always presupposes substantive value judgments and can succeed only to the extent that they are shared by the participants. The individuals involved must assume their places in the language-game and thus take part in a certain form of life. Shared values are presupposed by or constitutive of what we mean by "ethical discussion."

This view is confirmed by a particularly clear passage in *Culture and Value*. Wittgenstein says,

> "Nothing we do can be defended absolutely and finally. But only by reference to something else that is not questioned. I.e. no reason can be given why you should act (or should have acted) *like this*, except that by doing so you bring about such and such a situation, which again has to be an aim you *accept*" (p. 16).

For Wittgenstein there is a logical gap between reasons and actions. Asked to explain why we act as we do, we can offer reasons; when these are rejected, however, nothing more can be said.[13] Reasons do not compel actions. Our value claims arise out of reactions of satisfaction or approval, and reasons elucidate the nature of the satisfying or approved object. Thus the presence of reasons in the ethical sphere presupposes felt satisfactions or reactions of approval and not vice versa. If there are to be reasons, there must be de facto common reactions. This suggests that anyone who claims, for example, that ethics is a matter of personal preferences or is subjective either succumbs to a conceptual confusion or takes a substantive position without expressing an opinion concerning the "grammar of ethical discourse." Since ethical discourse is made possible by common reactions, it is simply a conceptual confusion to charge that it is subjective. There might, of course, not have been such agreements, and if there had not been, there would be no ethical discourse. But nothing in relation to this is a matter for conceptual analysis. Ethical discourse is possible only for people belonging to a community. It cannot begin in absolute value neutrality. We are interested beings, and only those interests and the activities to which they give rise enable us to share a language of evaluation.

It is no accident, therefore, that our preferences are, to a large extent, reflections of communal possibilities. We speak a language that is not our personal possession. It existed before we did and will continue to exist after we die. It provides us with ways of thinking that are not exclusively our own. We function in and are shaped by a social world already constituted by practices and activities that give form to our actions, thoughts, and feelings. Only by becoming parties to them can we put our own stamp on them. For this reason we are wrong if we think of individual preferences, reactions, or satisfactions as prior to our social setting. It may well be true that all valuing is individual, yet individuals are social in their constitution. Moral thinking thus does not begin from some value neutral ground. Rather it begins in and with the actual concerns and preferences of individuals, as these reflect the complex interplay between ways of speaking, ways of acting, and institutional arrangements all of which, together with our abilities and reactions, constitute "this human form of life."[14]

If, for Wittgenstein, ethical thinking is not a rationally compelling neutral ground but presupposes a substantive value position built on common reactions, should we not investigate those reactions? He considers this possibility in part 2 of *Philosophical Investigations* but rejects it.

> If the formation of concepts can be explained by facts of nature, should we not be interested, not in grammar, but rather in that in nature which is the basis of grammar?—Our interest certainly includes the correspondence between concepts

and very general facts of nature. . . . But our interest does not fall back upon these possible causes of the formation of concepts; we are not doing natural science." (230)[15]

Psychology or anthropology may present interesting facts concerning the formation of particular concepts. In fact, some such findings are obvious. Eskimos, as has been pointed out, have a number of distinct concepts for what we call "snow." But Wittgenstein is not interested in such empirical questions. He wants, rather, to break the hold a certain picture of the relation between concepts and facts has on us.

> If anyone believes that certain concepts are absolutely the correct ones, and that having different ones would mean not realizing something that we realize—then let him imagine certain very general facts of nature to be different from what we are used to, and the formation of concepts different from the usual ones will become intelligible to him. (*PI,* part 2, 230)

Wittgenstein's concern seems to end with displacing the idea that any concepts are "absolutely the correct ones." But he goes on to suggest a provocative comparison. "Compare a concept with a style of painting. For is even our style of painting arbitrary? Can we choose one at pleasure? (The Egyptian, for instance.) Is it a mere question of pleasing and ugly?" (*PI,* part 2, 230). The possibility Wittgenstein rejects here is that we might somehow step out of our own historical moment to choose another set of concepts or another style. Our appreciation of the Egyptian style depends completely on its being recognized as just that, a style. But how far are we to take this comparison? We know, for example, that though we may not be able to adopt a style at will, there is, nonetheless, a history of style, and some individuals—Giotto and Monet, for example—have contributed to important transformations within it. We know it makes no sense to suppose that such contributors produced something "absolutely correct." Yet they managed to advance matters by overcoming tensions and problems in previous styles.

The comparison between concepts and painting styles suggests a provocative line of thought for an understanding of ethical discourse.

Wittgenstein's other discussions appeal to "general facts of nature" and to "natural history," but the comparison with painting style brings in human history.[16] The context of natural history allows us to see the contingency of our practices. By interesting contrast, the comparison with painting locates our practices within a humanly constructed, changing history.

The instructive point of the comparison is that it identifies our morality as a particular evaluative stance among others, any of which can be called into question. This moves morality from being the context in which evaluation takes place to being an object of evaluation. Would Wittgenstein see the idea that morality is a specific evaluative stance presupposing common reactions that might have been otherwise and that might well change as opening a space in which to subject our ethical practices to assessment?

He would, we think, have rejected the possibility and, with it, the whole project of assessment, as products of what he calls the "main current of European and American civilization."[17] About this civilization Wittgenstein says: "Progress is its form rather than making progress one of its features." With apparent sadness, he remarks, "even clarity is sought only as a means to an end, not as an end in itself. For me on the contrary clarity, perspicuity are valuable in themselves." (*CV*, p. 6–7) It seems that for him the task of philosophy has come to an end once we "command a clear view of the use of our words" (*PI*, 122). After all,

> Philosophy may in no way interfere with the actual use of language; it can in the end only describe it. For it cannot give it a foundation either. It leaves everything as it is. It also leaves mathematics as it is . . . (*PI*, 124).

If philosophy leaves mathematics as it is, surely it also leaves ethics in the same position.[18] What does this mean? Wittgenstein rejects the idea that our practices require the sort of foundations traditional philosophy has sought to supply in the mistaken belief that without them what we do is questionable or problematic. If we take "philosophy" to mean the various methods employed in *Philosophical Investigations* to help us overcome the above mistake, then it must clearly leave everything as it is. Its task is completed when we are returned to our practices free of the persistent demands of traditional philosophy.[19]

Does this mean that there is no reflective criticism that can be brought to bear on our practices? There is, of course, no neutral perspective from which to launch such a critique, but the supposition that only such a critique would do is itself a prejudice of traditional philosophy. Any assessment has to be rooted in values. We cannot find a transcendental perch from which to examine our practices in their totality, but we can begin to see how they impinge on each other and how they enrich or diminish the quality of our lives. Perhaps Wittgenstein would not engage in this sort of criticism, but at least he leads us to the door behind which the possibility lies.

In contrast with Wittgenstein's reluctance to speak directly to issues of morality, Santayana addresses them happily and often. Strikingly, however, his attitude to the normative element in ethics shows as much distance and reticence as does Wittgenstein's. The reason is not an unwillingness on Santayana's part to make normative judgments, but his keen awareness that even at their best, they are *his* judgments only and hence fall short of universal validity. Philosophy, and with it ethics, Santayana says at the beginning of *Scepticism and Animal Faith,* begins in medias res[20] not only because we cannot escape our social and historical situatedness, but also because individuals constitute relative centers in a centerless world.

The rejection of universalist claims constitutes the negative side of Santayana's agreement with Wittgenstein concerning morality. Both resist the ideas that the same good can satisfy everyone and that all of us should pursue the same ideals. Santayana's reasoning in support of their shared view is more ontological and more clearly situated in the context of the history of philosophy than is Wittgenstein's, but the ultimate positions and their implications are virtually indistinguishable.

Santayana starts from the Aristotelian idea that nature determines perfection. What we value and what we do flow naturally from the sort of creatures we are. Without a definite constitution, nothing is better than anything else; who we are defines the excellence we can reach and what in the end satisfies us.

The Greeks were wrong only in supposing that human nature is single and immutable. Santayana calls this notion an "illusion" that "warped the moral impartiality" of their precepts (*RB,* pp. 480–81). He attempts to avoid the pitfall by being exquisitely sensitive to differences among humans. He goes so far as to toy with the idea that moral excellence is specific not only to species but to individuals, as well. The foundation of this position is his conviction that the ground of value is preference, and preference derives from the vital impulses of the organism. This means that the individual psyche, "the hereditary principle of organization in the body or of direction in the will" (*RB,* p. 481), is the ultimate source and arbiter of the good.

He returns to the idea that "actual preference has its only possible seat" in the individual organism again and again. Since "the root of morality is animal bias," we must look to the physically integrated, insular body if we wish to understand its nature. For ease of reference, Santayana calls the body's dynamic internal structure "psyche," the Greek term for soul. The unity the name suggests is mythological, the result of our reading purposes into the movement of the physical world, yet the swirling processes of which this material self consists are real, defining our potentialities and needs. The psyche is a self-sustaining vortex compelled "to care, to watch, to pursue, and to possess"; its needs and weaknesses make its life one of constant selectivity (*RB,* pp. 481, 483, 341).

This selectivity, the preferring of one alternative to innumerable others, is the organic ground or counterpart of valuation. Although its objects extend beyond the narrowly physical to the realm of ideal allegiances, its presence reveals the work of organized life. Santayana is tempted to think that values are individual because he believes that they arise from biological organisms and notes that each animal body is an independently operating agent. The differences among these agents define the differences of their goods; there can be no values beyond those established by the needs and preferences of individuals.

Such a view renders the possibility of universal moral claims dependent on the empirical presence of universal similarities. Since the sphere of values is restricted to needy, desirous, operating organisms, we must search for the common good in the resembling natures of individual persons. This, to be sure, avoids relativisms of the standard sort, for it makes the good a function not of the temporary opinions or passing wants of the creature, but of its continuing or permanent nature. It is, in that respect, simply Aristotle's view of virtue as excellence of action grounded in habits, stripped of its incidental and questionable commitments to the fixity of species and the uniformity of human perfection.

Individual relationalism of this sort concerning the good has two significant outcomes. First, it calls on us to be tolerant of alien values and to permit, so long as they do not interfere with our own fulfillment, as wide a variety of divergent lives to flourish as nature might generate. And even when we enter combat on behalf of what we consider the right and the good, the belief that each constitution has its own perfection should enable us to rise above narrow partiality at least on the level of understanding. In a characteristically elegant passage, Santayana declares:

> Real unselfishness consists in sharing the interests of others. Beyond the pale of actual unanimity the only possible unselfishness is chivalry—a recognition of the inward right and justification of our enemies fighting against us. This chivalry has long been practiced in the battle-field without abolishing the causes of war; and it might conceivably be extended to all the conflicts of men with one another, and of the warring elements within each breast. (WD, p. 151)

A sound assessment of the source and scope of the validity of our own commitments opens the door, in this way, to raising ourselves above ethical absolutism, which is but "the mental grimace of passion" (WD, p. 152). Keeping the living context of values uppermost in our minds helps us remember that, in the moral life at least, critique from an external point of view is always irrelevant. It may also lead to an understanding of why universal prescriptions are not only inappropriate, but in the end also useless. Shared values require shared natures. Such natures are shared not as essentialists would have it, by identical possession of some generic feature, but in the nominalistic way Wittgenstein outlined in his discussion of family resemblances.[21]

The second consequence of Santayana's individual relationalism concerns the power, or we should perhaps say poverty, of philosophy. He clearly shares Wittgenstein's suspicion of philosophers in their self-professed role as arbiters of knowledge and value. With respect to the good, in particular, no grand discovery is to be expected of them. We must not look to them even for insightful general examinations of the value of what people value, for the simple reason that there are no universal principles to ground such critiques. If private nature determines private good, moral evaluation becomes an individualistic affair dispersed among a multitude of different centers of striving connected at most by loose family resemblances.

As tolerant minds have suspected throughout the history of thought, the job of philosophers is to try to understand all and to leave everything pretty much unchanged. Wholesale critique based on judgment out of context misses the uniqueness and internal integrity of every nature. Enhancement of the good is possible only by entering the soul with sympathy in order to help it clarify its allegiances and identify its long-term interests. Though philosophers are supposed to be lovers of wisdom, they cannot do this much better than sensitive and caring ordinary people; at any rate, nothing in their education prepares them to help others, or even themselves, purify ideals, embrace them unambiguously and focus dispersed energies on attaining them.

The task of philosophy, then, is largely negative. It must recognize the irreducible multiplicity of values and warn against the dangers of totalizing dogmatism. It must resist the temptation to suppose that there are universal standards to be developed and justified. Most important, it must control its unquenchable thirst for elevating one set of practices and its attendant goods to ideal status. Recognition of the integrity of multiform perfections is, to be sure, a positive result. But just as "Buy low, sell high!" says nothing concretely about how to invest, so feasting one's eyes on the many forms of the good makes no useful contribution to how anyone should live. Philosophy must learn to be modest about what it can achieve.

We said that Santayana *toys* with the sort of individual relationalism we have just described because, in important respects, it is not his final and deliberate position. Nevertheless, he likes the idea; it seems to speak to him in a deeply personal way. Santayana and Wittgenstein were intensely private individuals. Although they understood the actual and the philosophical significance of social life, they always viewed it from the standpoint of their emotional isolation. Santayana permitted this perspective to penetrate his philosophical reflections much more than did Wittgenstein. He is at his rhetorical best when he writes of the lone person facing the challenge of an alien world or seeking inner peace. His stress on the insular individual makes him the only major American philosopher whose work invites comparison with the existentialists.

Although the image of isolated persons seeking their special perfections attracts Santayana profoundly, he knows that it is not a sound representation of how the moral life operates. To be sure, there are some value differences among people, reflecting disparities in nature. But the differences in values and in natures pale by comparison with the similarities. The structure and predispositions of the organism resemble those of its forebears. Society builds personalities out of and to top off these biological endowments. Social construction aims at creating relatively uniform persons, people who share habits and values and who respond to the same incentives. The fact that human natures can endure only as individuated psyches does not mean that they constitute independent or isolated individuals.

We must pay particular attention to the socialization that creates natures for the young. Through formal education, child-rearing routines and informal examples set by peers, we replicate the dominant habits and appraisals of the group. The same propagation of established values occurs each time a person decides to join some association or accepts a job. Natures are constructed through communal practices, many of which define and embody values internal to them.

Once we recognize that Santayana does not think values are the outcome of untutored instinct, we can see the powerful positive side of his agreement with Wittgenstein. The negative aspect of their accord was the rejection of universal claims about the good. Positively, they concur in the belief that moral life and moral values reside in particular social practices. "All morality is deeply social," Santayana announces, and proceeds to show that "morality in general . . . is no morality at all" (*RB,* p. 482). Though its elements are physical, the psyche itself is a social creature, constituted by the practices of the community that rears it. Consequently, the ultimately relevant relation defining the good is not that of the world or relevant parts of it to an unsituated organism, but to a being enmeshed in social, historical and cultural contexts.

Santayana never surrenders the idea that "The biological unit is the individual body, the spiritual unit is the individual soul" (*POML,* p. 195) but his insistence is best understood as a reaction against the Hegelian excess of supposing that societies or states are organic beings. In fact, they are institutions, not animals and are, therefore, ill adapted or unable to sustain the focused life of action required by morality.[22] Once we examine the nature of any psyche, however, we see upon it the marks of the habits and practices of its social world. Its good derives in large part from its participation in these activities.

This point is made by Santayana with unmistakable clarity in a passage, published posthumously, about the development of morality: "The good itself assumes a different form when a different art is employed to pursue it. The thrifty mind, the pugnacious mind, and the religious mind cease to exist at once or by turns in the same person. They dominate different classes; until the warrior thinks it beneath him to labour, and the priest thinks it a virtue in himself not to fight" (*POML,* p. 202). Practice and its context define virtue and it is futile trying to impose the good intrinsic to one manner of operating on the practitioners of another. Although, being unwilling to accord central significance to language, Santayana does not speak of these modes of operation as language-games, it is clear that what he has in mind closely resembles the structured activities Wittgenstein calls by that name. Our practices and their broad natural context constitute, for both Santayana and Wittgenstein, our shared form of life.

If we wish to know the good of participating psyches, we must understand their structuring social activities. Individual relationalism becomes, in this way, a sort of practice-relationalism. Each of the practices involved has its own integrity and cannot be trumped by bickering objections from the standpoint of other, even rival, practices. In agreement with Wittgenstein, Santayana does not exclude the possibility of critique, only of one based on neutral or universal principles.

We may pass judgment, for example, on the ways in which practices conflict and thus fail to contribute to the realization of broader purposes. Such judgments, however, themselves presuppose value commitments. Santayana gave a great deal of attention to the notion of a life of reason that aims at the harmonious satisfaction of the largest possible number of our impulses. It may seem that such a universal rule demanding that we maximize the good is a compulsory neutral principle of sanity. But, he says,

> Even the most general and tolerant of moral standards—harmony—is not a good in itself. There must be an actual will directed upon harmony in order to render harmony a good. Harmony demands many a sacrifice: in what direction, and at whose cost, shall those sacrifices be made? A strong and well-knit nature, brave with the perfect harmony within, will despise and detest harmony on a larger scale; it will refuse to sacrifice any part of its chosen good, and will declare eternal war on the devil, and on all his obsequious and insidious agents.[23]

Even reason and the harmony it extols are values, then, only if chosen. We can change our commitments, but never step outside the partiality values impose so as to gain a transcendent perspective that reveals the "real" good. We can criticize values, but only from the standpoint of other values that remain, for the moment, uncriticized. But it is important to recognize that often there is little point to carping at the goods whose pursuit engages other people. Why try to convince the rugby team to spend the afternoon reading Walter Pater? Whether we call them language-games, forms of life, practices or animal activities, our multiform occupations focus our energies and engross the soul. If they satisfy, it is best to leave them unchanged.

Chapter 4

FORMS OF LIFE AND ANIMAL FAITH

Both Wittgenstein and Santayana contend that philosophy can be honest only by taking account of the living context in which thought occurs. This is what Wittgenstein calls our "form of life." The notion is difficult to explicate, at least partly because Wittgenstein himself says very little about it. But we will argue that it is of fundamental importance for understanding Wittgenstein's idea of the enterprise of philosophy. Only by locating language, and with it thought, within our forms of life can he avoid the transcendental character of the *Tractatus Logico-Philosophicus*. And only by seeing the role this notion plays in setting the ultimate context of our practices do we fully grasp the way Wittgenstein thinks philosophy can be done.

Wittgenstein regularly reminds us of the larger context in which language has its place. But this larger context is not a single structure, not something fixed and unchanging. Its salient feature is sometimes the broader activity in which a language-game operates and at others certain of our characteristics as human animals active in a world that our language and actions take for granted. These activities and these characteristics constitute the forms life takes; since they are not always the same activities and the same characteristics, the forms are numerous and do not constitute even a complex unitary way of living or being in the world.[1]

There are only five occurrences of the term "form(s) of life" in *Philosophical Investigations*, but a careful examination of them will allow us to see what Wittgenstein has in mind and to gain a better understanding of his other texts. Let us examine them one at a time.

Wittgenstein uses the term for the first time in paragraph 19, where he writes, "It is easy to imagine a language consisting only of orders and reports in battle.—Or a language consisting only of questions and expressions for answering yes and no. And innumerable others.—And to imagine a language means to imagine a form of life." Here the term functions to bring to the forefront the idea that language is situated within a larger context of activities. To imagine a language, then, is to imagine speaking or writing within that context, playing a role and making a difference in the lives of those involved in the activities.

If we keep such integrated activity in mind, the term "language-game" can be misleading. In stressing the term "game," we may be led to think of an activity that is isolated from the rest of what we do. To play baseball, for example, is to engage in an activity that is structured and rule-governed but that does not impact our lives outside the game.[2] We cannot do anything with runs after the game is over. We say, "It is just a game," meaning that it is not of lasting importance or that its outcome makes no real difference. When Wittgenstein stresses the gamelike character of our linguistic practices, he certainly does not mean to suggest anything like this. Because language is embedded in what we do—in our practices as builders, for example—what we say does make a difference. So, to imagine a language is to imagine the practice of which it is a part. It is to imagine a form that life might or actually does take. In this way, language is conceived as naturally situated in the midst of activities and things. Just as we must not think of the meaning of a term as isolated from the use of the other terms that function in a language-game, so we must not isolate the language-game from the larger context in which it occurs.

Language is not primarily a syntactical structure to be mapped onto the world; Wittgenstein radically reconceived "the problem of meaning" from the days of the *Tractatus*. There language was understood as a structured set of signs that, to have meaning, must stand in a suitable relation to items in the world. In *Philosophical Investigations,* by contrast, we are offered a much richer understanding of language, one that sees it as already part of the world or, more properly, already a part of the range of activities in which human beings engage.[3]

The second occurrence of "form of life" repeats the key points we have just made. Wittgenstein asks,

> But how many kinds of sentence are there? Say assertion, question and command?—There are *countless* kinds: countless different kinds of use of what we call "symbols," "words," "sentences." And this multiplicity is not something fixed, given once for all; but new types of language, new language-games, as we may say, come into existence, and others become obsolete and get forgotten. (We can get a *rough picture* of this from the changes in mathematics.)
>
> Here the term "language-*game*" is meant to bring into prominence the fact that the *speaking* of language is part of an activity, or of a form of life. (*PI*, 23)

To understand language is to understand it as part of the activities in which it is embedded. We cannot isolate it from the rich diversity of human practices. At the end of this section, Wittgenstein explicitly rejects his earlier unidimensional view by saying "it is interesting to compare the multiplicity of the tools in language . . . with what logicians have said about the structure of language. (Including the author of the *Tractatus Logico-Philosophicus*.)" (*PI*, 23).

These two opening uses serve, among other things, to underline the fundamental shift that has occurred between Wittgenstein's early and his later thinking. Language is a living thing embedded in human activities and must be understood as an organic part of those activities. This idea accounts for much of Wittgenstein's philosophical method in his later work. He thinks that the proper way to correct the misunderstandings of philosophers is to describe the role a troublesome or misleading stretch of language has in our activities and thereby to gain what he calls a "perspicuous representation" (*PI*, 122). These descriptions take their point from the philosophical problems that puzzle us and are meant to let us see how philosophers have forgotten or misconceived the situated character of language.[4] These first two uses of the phrase do not suggest anything as grandiose or totalizing as *the* "human form of life." The meaning of "form of life" in these two passages is quite mundane. A form of life is simply the wider, generally nonlinguistic context in which language has its home.

"Form of life" also occurs in a passage we have already discussed in some detail. This use introduces a subtle new twist on the earlier theme. Although reference to "form of life" continues to have the function of situating language in a broader context, here it does so by focusing on the relations of language to its users—human beings. At no. 241, Wittgenstein contrasts agreement in opinion and agreement in form of life. What he has in mind, as we have already seen, is a contrast between de facto similarities among human beings in virtue of which they share a common language and the opinions formulated within that language on which they might agree.

Human beings are alike in certain important respects, and Wittgenstein calls such resemblances to our attention as a way of situating our linguistic practices. He sees these similarities as grounding language, or making it possible. He describes this in the following way: "What we are supplying are really remarks on the natural history of human beings; we are not contributing curiosities however, but observations which no one has doubted, but which have escaped remark only because they are always before our eyes" (*PI*, 415). Here the stress is on what might broadly be called the *human* form of life. Language is a tool used by human beings and as such it is fitted to utilize the capacities and meet the needs of those who use it. It is important to note that Wittgenstein does not speak of social but of natural history, whose processes develop over a long time and change very slowly. These common features of language users provide the context in which the structures of language can be understood.

This is the place to try to make sense of Wittgenstein's enigmatic remark in *Philosophical Investigations* that if a lion could speak, we could not understand it (*PI*, part 2, 223). Since "the common behavior of mankind is the system of reference by means of which we interpret an unknown language" (*PI*, 206), to take the sounds of a lion as language in the full sense of the word would be to interpret its linguistic behavior in human terms. But a lion's responses are not human responses, so we do not have a system of reference by which to interpret them. Yet, we might ask, is a lion so different from us? Can we not make some sense of its actions? And if we can, do we not, at least to some extent, share a form of life with it?[5]

There is something strange and paradoxical about this contention, as there is with a number of Wittgenstein's other remarks. We might well suppose that if we knew that a lion was *speaking,* it would at least be possible for us to understand it. For to identify sounds as speech is to set them in a frame of reference. To be able to distinguish between random sounds, animal responses (such as the barking of dogs), and articulate speech is already to have understood a great deal. So if a lion did indeed *speak,* it seems that we would be able to understand it. Or, at the very least, the difficulty in understanding it would be of the sort we had with translating Linear B.[6]

The paradoxical appearance arises because we want to think of two distinct moments in the process: one of identifying sounds as speech and a second of providing a translation. But these are not hermetically sealed domains. Speech must have intimate and intricate connections to the nonverbal behavior of the speaker, as is the case with humans, and to know these connections is to know much about the creature speaking. So the ultimate point Wittgenstein may be making is that there cannot be an untranslatable language except in the simple sense that we might never be able to pull off its translation because we know too little about the place of the words in the lives of those who use them. In the case of creatures like ourselves, even if we do not know many specific things about other speakers, there is a great deal we share with them because of our common human form of life. The background similarities go unremarked precisely because they are always before our eyes. Only when we forget them are we tempted to see language as something "surrounded by a halo" or as in need of justification and of no use to us without philosophical grounding.

The next reference to forms of life strengthens the interpretation we are offering. Wittgenstein says,

One can imagine an animal angry, frightened, unhappy, happy, startled. But hopeful? And why not?

A dog believes his master is at the door. But can he also believe his master will come the day after to-morrow?—And *what* can he not do here?—How do I do it?—How am I supposed to answer this?

Can only those hope who can talk? Only those who have mastered the use of a language. That is to say, the phenomena of hope are modes of this complicated form of life. (If a concept refers to a character of human handwriting, it has no application to beings that do not write). (*PI*, 174)

It is no accident that the dog cannot hope or believe that his master will come the day after tomorrow. What in the animal's behavior would allow us to distinguish between believing that his master will come the day after tomorrow and that he will come two weeks from now? To suppose that such a distinction is possible for the dog would involve attributing a rich conceptual life to it, yet one that is never exhibited in anything the dog does. It does not make sense to introduce such a rift between the cognitive life and the overt behavior of the animal, particularly if we wish to situate thought and language within a natural setting. When Wittgenstein says that the phenomena of hope are modes of "this complicated form of life,"[7] a life that involves complex linguistic behaviors, he is referring to the way humans live in and through their communicative practices and the commonalities these presuppose.[8]

The final place in which the term "form of life" occurs in *Philosophical Investigations* is another passage we have already discussed. On p. 226 of Part II, Wittgenstein says, "What has to be accepted, the given, is—so one could say—*forms of life.*"

We should remark at once that we do not think it very important whether Wittgenstein uses the singular or plural of "form of life." Sometimes he stresses particular facts about ourselves, and each of these can be seen as a "form" human life takes. Viewed in this way, there are many forms of life. On other occasions, he stresses comprehensive human commonalities and speaks of form of life in the singular. This is not a matter of philosophical substance.

We have already noted that with the comment just quoted Wittgenstein wishes to reject the traditional epistemological project of finding or constructing foundations. He puts in its place the descriptive enterprise that locates our complex linguistic practices in a human situatedness stretching from our de facto agreement in making color judgments to the shared unreflective (what Wittgenstein calls "natural") responses we make to pleasures and pains. When he asks, "Are we perhaps over-hasty in our assumption that the smile of an unweaned infant is not a pretense?—And on what experience is our assumption based?" (*PI*, 249), he is making a comment on what is "given"—the form of life we inhabit.

> But how *can* previous experience be a ground for assuming that such-and-such will occur later on?—the answer is: What general concept have we of grounds for this kind of assumption? This sort of statement about the past is simply what we call a ground for assuming that this will happen in the future.—And if you are surprised at our playing such a game I refer you to the *effect* of a past experience (to the fact that a burnt child fears the fire). (*PI*, 480)

The skeptical question with which this passage begins presupposes that we have some notion of "ground" that is independent of our actual procedures of inductive reasoning. Since within those procedures "this sort of statement about the past is simply what we call a ground," the question assumes the possibility of standing outside the practices in which our terms have meaning. But if the term "ground" is not a part of such a practice, what right do we have to suppose that it bears any relation to our activities? So either the skeptic's "doubt" is misplaced, for there is no room for it within the language-game, or it is irrelevant because it does not relate to our practices. A practice in which what Wittgenstein here calls "a general concept of 'ground'" has a place would simply be a different practice from any we have. It would therefore play a different role in the lives of those who participate in it, even though it may be difficult to imagine what role that could be.

Wittgenstein's typical mode of argument begins with a description of the language-game we play, showing that in that game there is no room for the skeptical question. Such descriptions have bite, however, only if we round out the account by reminding ourselves that the game is played by creatures of a particular sort and that it is not a mere game in the usual sense of the term. Situating the language-game in the economy of the life of such creatures shows its function. That is what Wittgenstein conveys when he says, "if you are surprised at our playing such a game [the one with terms such as "ground"] I refer you to the *effect* of a past experience (to the fact that a burnt child fears the fire)."

This is a particularly clear example of Wittgenstein's thinking. Traditional philosophical problems are seen to presuppose a sort of transcendent standpoint, the very possibility of which is rejected. We are reminded of how we actually use the word in question or play the game. Within that game, there is simply no room for the question the philosopher wants to raise, and for that reason the question is nonsensical. But our practices are not left hanging. We can come to a fuller understanding of what goes on by seeing them in context—by seeing them in the light of certain facts about ourselves. "I shall get burnt if I put my hand in the fire: that is certainty. That is to say: here we see the meaning of certainty. (What it amounts to, not just the meaning of the word 'certainty.')" For creatures like ourselves for whom "the belief that fire will burn me is of the same kind as the fear that it will burn me" (*PI*, 474, 473), it is no mere speculation that previous experience is a ground for thinking that such-and-such will occur later on. Thus Wittgenstein completes his discussions by locating the practice in question within a larger frame that includes obvious but overlooked facts about ourselves. In short he reminds us of the form of life we keep.

As we noted earlier, we should not suppose that the features Wittgenstein identifies as aspects of our form of life are uniquely human. In fact, in a striking passage in *On Certainty* he says,

One might say: "'I know' expresses *comfortable* certainty, not the certainty that is still struggling."

Now I would like to regard this certainty, not as something akin to hastiness or superficiality, but as a form of life. (That is very badly expressed and probably badly thought as well.)

But that means I want to conceive it as something that lies beyond being justified or unjustified; as it were, as something animal (357–59).

We are animals engaged in and with a world that responds to our actions differentially and to varying degrees. The child burnt by fire who then fears it is a paradigm of this engagement. Its response is recognizable as a basic human/animal one. It is prior to or independent of justification and gives meaning to such key terms as "certainty." The human animal's certainty about its world as a field of engagement and about the behavior of relevant parts of it is an expression of its form of life. That engagement and its success give meaning to the practices in which we participate.

If we forget the larger context, we isolate our practices and rob them of their function or point. This makes it appear that they need to be justified, even while it renders all attempts at justification futile. Languages are spoken by living creatures in the context of making their way in the world. If we forget this, we can understand nothing. We must always keep in mind that, as Wittgenstein puts it, to imagine a language is to imagine a form of life.

Although it is worth repeating that Santayana's discussion of major philosophical issues never pivots on his view of language, he nevertheless makes a number of points that bear a striking resemblance to the views of Wittgenstein. This is particularly true with respect to the nature and significance of forms of life and to the relevance of this notion to the work of philosophy.

When Santayana rejects the search for the sort of certainty only immediate presence provides, he does so in the name of honesty in philosophical reflection. "Philosophy is nothing if not honest," he announces (*SAF,* p. 187). This requires admission that we cannot attain incontrovertible knowledge and recognition that we do not need it for the purposes of life. Since even skeptics leave their doubts behind when they go to the dinner table, is it not reasonable to be intellectually satisfied with the sort and level of assurance that suffices for successful operation in the world? Such certainty can, of course, always be assailed from the standpoint of stricter standards: we can be invited to quiver at the idea that we may be wrong about everything and to contemplate the dreadful consequences of the notion that the falsity of all we firmly believe is a genuine, though perhaps only a logical, possibility.

But what is the source and legitimacy of such stricter standards? Wittgenstein sees them as nonsensical or illegitimate because they have no place in the language-games we play and in our broader practices of which they are parts. Santayana argues that they are irrelevant or illegitimate because they are unconnected to what we do in the processes of ordinary living. These processes define who we are and constitute our form of life. They show that we are neither pure intellects engaged in investigation for its own sake nor puzzled minds intent on escaping deception at all costs. We are instead embodied and socially situated animals operating in a treacherous environment. Inquiry has its point and origin in dealing with our needs and in fending off the blows of a cruel world. Doubt also has a function, but only in the actual and concrete circumstances of managing contingencies.

In the language of the philosophical tradition that Santayana never hesitates to adopt, animal life with its inevitable belief structure enjoys existential primacy in the human world. We are, first and foremost, social animals in busy pursuit of our purposes. Our habits and practices are focused on the attainment of practical ends, on making our engagement with the world as satisfactory as possible. Neither Wittgenstein nor Santayana thinks it appropriate to go into detail on the specific purposes underlying what we do and on the criteria of satisfaction. The significant philosophical move is to accept and acknowledge that we are animals engaged in social practices aimed at objectives connected with life and fulfillment.

Forms of Life and Animal Faith

Santayana believes that whatever has existential primacy should enjoy epistemic prerogatives as well. Accordingly his philosophy of animal faith embraces the engaged life of the animal as its foundation. Of course, we must not suppose that he takes "foundation" to mean the absolutely certain ground of all further knowledge. What he has in mind instead is simply the actual starting point of philosophical reflection, the "given" reality that makes the investigative process possible and serves, at the same time, as its object. The fact that Santayana thinks of our form of life as the beginning of reflection while Wittgenstein uses it as its final stage should not, moreover, be seen as a significant difference between them. They agree that whether you start or end with the facts of animal life, they constitute the final and definitive context of all our practices.

Wittgenstein's desire to end with reference to our form of life may well be an expression of his reluctance to construct positive philosophical accounts. He asserts that such forms are the ultimate factual limits to our queries and puzzlements, but he leaves open their precise nature and variety. His investigation comes to rest in saying that a certain language-game is part of a way of life; it is as though at that point nothing further needs to be said either about the language-game or about the final reality it expresses. Santayana takes animal life no less as a given. But he sees in its brute facticity an occasion to enhance and systematize our understanding of the world. Accordingly he proceeds to present an organized account of the tenets of animal faith, that is, of the beliefs we are justified in holding because, as animals, we act them out.

The purpose of adopting animal life as the ultimate given is conservative in both Santayana and Wittgenstein. Both wage war, after all, on the pretensions of traditional philosophy, and both want to affirm the legitimacy of our ordinary practices. They want to show that life as we lead it is immune to the wholesale criticism of intellectuals and that the enterprise of challenging everything is radically misconceived. They accomplish their purpose by focusing on different targets: Wittgenstein shows the coherence of ordinary language and delegitimates philosophical extensions of it, while Santayana displays the coherence of ordinary beliefs and delegitimates philosophical challenges to them. The unity of their aims, their claims, their strategies, and their results overshadows their differences over the desirability of modest philosophical constructions.

Santayana proposes just such a modest structure in his philosophy of animal faith. The idea is that we must come "to rest at some point upon vulgar faith." Since philosophy is "only convention made consistent and deliberate," its job is to survey and systematize the beliefs we find inevitably involved in what we do (*SAF*, pp. 187, 186). By "convention" in this context, Santayana does not mean the outcome of agreement or the sum of dispensable social customs, but rather what people believe as a result of living in the world and silently concur that it is sensible to believe. We do not need elaborate surveys and questionnaires to identify these opinions; examining our actions to see what commitments are implicated in them is enough. These tenets constitute "the shrewd orthodoxy" of the human race.

Just as Wittgenstein claims to be assembling reminders of what we already know,[9] Santayana says that he "can only spread a feast of what everybody knows." Everyone is a realist in behavior: we all believe that "there is a world, that there is a future, that things sought can be found, and things seen can be eaten" (*SAF*, pp. ix, 180). These are the "original articles of the animal creed"—we simply cannot act without tacitly assuming their truth. We believe them, even if we are not always fully conscious of the beliefs and an abstract formulation of them might appear puzzling. If, in searching for the milk in the refrigerator, we were confronted by someone who exclaimed, "So you think the milk exists independently of you and even though you don't now see it!" we might well wonder what in the world he or she had in mind. But if we disregard the motivation behind saying such things, the only proper answer is, "Of course, silly." We all believe these matters, and we act on the beliefs; without such commitments and such actions, animal life would be impossible.

Although Wittgenstein is at odds with such uses of the word "believe," the difference between him and Santayana is, once again, less than it at first appears. For, when all is said and done, believing the "tenets" of animal faith is, in Santayana's view, simply acting on them; the belief, as Peirce never tired of saying, *is* the habit of action.

Forms of Life and Animal Faith

So whether one tries to give philosophical voice to our shared practices, as does Santayana, or drowns philosophical controversies in them, as does Wittgenstein, the centrality of what we do for what we should think stands as a common foundation. Wittgenstein may have had this final ground of thought in mind when he said: "If one tried to advance *theses* in philosophy, it would never be possible to question them, because everyone would agree to them" (*PI*, 128).

Santayana concurs with the sentiment that there would be no disagreement if philosophy were done properly. He begins the preface to *Scepticism and Animal Faith* by saying, "Here is one more system of philosophy. If the reader is tempted to smile I can assure him that I smile with him. . . . I am merely attempting to express for the reader the principles to which he appeals when he smiles" (*SAF*, p. v). Although he develops a vocabulary in which he can articulate the "principles" behind the smile, he recognizes the tenuous character of any such project. The central difference between his views and those of Wittgenstein is that he thinks there is value in focusing our minds on the substantive points about animal life concerning which there is general agreement. Wittgenstein, by contrast, sees philosophy more negatively, as an activity whose purpose is to liberate us from the bewitchment of language, from the compulsion to wrench words out of their everyday use and context.

Detailing the agreements is important at least in part because it establishes the parameters of philosophy, closing off the possibility of skeptical doubts and metaphysical constructions. It is of further significance because the ubiquity of animal commitments makes them invisible; they escape "remark only because they are always before our eyes" (*PI*, 415). But Santayana sees yet another reason for the systematic exposition of the tenets of our form of life. The function of philosophy is in the end moral and spiritual. Its job is to help us lead a life worthy of human beings: "Mind was not created for the sake of discovering the absolute truth. . . . The function of mind is rather to increase the wealth of the universe in the spiritual dimension, by adding appearance to substance and passion to necessity, and by creating all those private perspectives, and those emotions of wonder, adventure, curiosity, and laughter which omniscience would exclude" (*RB*, p. xiii). Understanding our practices and acknowledging our common life guide us in the direction of what we already know to be, but have not yet consciously embraced as, the truly satisfying.

Accordingly Santayana fills out the "original articles of the animal creed" with a list of beliefs acted out in daily life. In addition to being convinced that there is a world, we also think there are enduring selves that seek their weal in it. The world consists, moreover, of elements that are unevenly distributed in space and that undergo relatively orderly change in time.[10] Some parts of our surroundings take the form of animals "in whom there are feelings, images, and thoughts" (*RB*, p. 233). These thoughts, when aptly symbolic, give animals knowledge of the operations of their environment and, when retrospective, a generally accurate though usually imprecise account of the past. That our ideas are not always correct suggests the existence of a truth independent of what we think but open to investigation, and the inquiries in which we engage presuppose that the minds of at least some animals are alert and intelligent.

How can one disagree with this summary account of what all of us know? It constitutes nothing more than a systematic description of the generic features of our form of life. This is how intelligent human life operates, and this human is at once also an animal life. We need do nothing further than acknowledge it and pursue it with good conscience. If anything is bedrock for philosophy, we have reached it here.

Santayana gives voice to traditional thought one more time and offers the following reflection: "It might seem ignominious to believe something on compulsion, because I can't help believing it; when reason awakes in a man it asks for reasons for everything. Yet this demand is unreasonable: there cannot be a reason for everything. It is mere automatic habit in the philosopher to make this demand, as it is in the common man not to make it" (*SAF*, p. 186). Just as there is always a last house on the street, so there must be a last explanation. When we say, "These are the facts; this is how we live," the affair is closed. The fact that our form of life has a certain structure does not mean that it is unchangeable. But changes come slowly in the course of animal life, and they are not brought about by the questionings or the wishes of philosophers.

Our job is to embrace the practices that constitute our form of life and have no concern about their legitimacy. Should change be possible and desirable, we could go about working for it, but that is not a philosophical issue. And the way change is to occur, if it can at all, is not open to philosophical direction. Philosophers must satisfy themselves, as Santayana thinks, with evoking some very general essences to sketch the outlines of our world. For the rest, as Wittgenstein maintains, philosophy must leave everything as it is.

The striking similarity of their positions leaves us with the urgent question of what more than style and emphasis separate the philosophies of Santayana and Wittgenstein. We may find a difference of substance in Santayana's devotion to transcendence in the form of the spiritual life. We turn next to exploring this interesting possibility.

Chapter 5

RELIGIOUS BELIEF

Freethinkers and critically minded intellectuals have raised questions about religion for thousands of years. Many of the critiques have been internal to the religions questioned, consisting of objections to or assessments of their sacred texts. Higher biblical criticism, for example, has been of this sort, inflicting significant damage on Judaism and Christianity, but offering little in the way of positive alternatives.

The development of science, especially of biology, presented established religion with a different and novel challenge. By the second half of the nineteenth century, human beings were in possession of an organized body of reasonably well-confirmed theories that seemed to be in direct conflict with the hallowed claims of Christianity. Taken at face value, religion maintained that the world was created in six days; physics and geology pointed to gradual development over billions of years. Religion asserted that human beings were immediate products of the divine will; biology and anthropology countered with evidence of the slow evolution of humans from earlier animal life forms.

The conflict burst into the open in England around 1870, when T. H. Huxley and other followers of Darwin engaged the bishops of the Church of England in bitter debate about which of the accounts was more worthy of belief. The devastating result changed our understanding of religion once and for all.

The evolutionists made it clear that when it comes to evidence in the ordinary sense of the term, religion has little or nothing to offer to derail the claims of science. Taken as a descriptive account of the origin of the world and of human beings, religion came to look like a set of outmoded conjectures or outright errors.

To avoid this fate, Christianity would have to give up its claim to literal truth, leaving explanations of the world of facts as the exclusive province of empirical science. This removed the conflict of science and religion, but it exacted a high price, relegating the claims of the soul and heart to a dubious, secondary status.

Subsequent interpretations of religious statements as symbolic were, accordingly, ambivalent concerning their value as cognitive claims. On the one hand, symbolic truths appeared deeper than the mundane variety. On the other hand, however, they seemed to be more and more like stories told us, as though we were children, to comfort us in the cold world.

Many of those who thought the only hope for saving religion was to reinterpret it as the symbolic expression of the travails of the human soul were not really sympathetic to its claims. They tended to view the symbolism in aesthetic terms, converting the living authority of faith to the integrity of a beautiful image and reducing its commands to tame recommendations. Few could understand the power and affirm the self-justifying independence of the religious life. Remarkably, without being religious themselves, Santayana and Wittgenstein were among those who did.

Throughout his life, Wittgenstein expressed considerable respect for religion and the religious, even in their most primitive forms.[1] He says, "The ways in which people have had to express their religious beliefs differ enormously. All genuine expressions of religion are wonderful, even those of the most savage peoples."[2] This deep respect, however, is not uncritical. Wittgenstein draws a careful distinction between religion and mere superstition. He remarks that "Religious faith and superstition are entirely different. One of them springs from fear and is a kind of false science. The other is trusting" (*CV*, p. 72). The distinction he has in mind is worked out in some detail in his *Remarks on Frazer's Golden Bough,* where he defends religious beliefs against the crude reductionism that sees them as forms of provisional or primitive science. He says,

Frazer's account of the magical and religious views of mankind is unsatisfactory; It makes these views look like *errors*. Was Augustine in error, then, when he called upon God on every page of the *Confessions?* But—one might say—if he was not in error, surely the Buddhist holy man was—or anyone else—whose religion gives expression to completely different views. But *none* of them was in error, except when he set forth a theory. (p. 119)

How can this be? Surely Christianity, at least, presupposes or implies a background metaphysics or, as Wittgenstein calls it here, a "theory," along with a collection of historical claims. It involves talk of God and of the afterlife, and such talk seems to presuppose supernaturalism and some sort of mind-body dualism, views clearly rejected by the later Wittgenstein. It also presents detailed accounts of the presumably historical deeds of Jesus.

Such a view of religion involves a particular and questionable stand with regard to the meaning of religious language. It assumes, in the words of Rush Rhees, that "the language of religion is . . . in some way comparable with the language in which one describes matters of fact."[3] The claims of religion are supposed to capture historical, physical, and metaphysical truths that may, unfortunately, exceed our cognitive powers but are nonetheless matters of objective fact. This way of understanding religious statements also commits us to a view of the nature of religious believing. If the "truths" of religion are matters of fact, then to believe is to give them intellectual assent. We may do this on faith and not on the basis of evidence, but belief here is of the same sort as in history or science.

We have already discussed Wittgenstein's rejection of the idea that language requires any sort of metaphysics; religious language presents no exception. He wants to see language as an aspect of a complicated form of life that conditions and is conditioned by what we are as human animals. This very project may, of course, be seen as contrary to important claims of the religious life. Do not many religions teach that to pay primary attention to such worldly situatedness is to misconceive our condition? Human life is not, after all, supposed to be limited to physical time and historical location. Our destiny is said to lie beyond. The religious believer might thus think that, since it presents religion as but an aspect of our secular form of life, Wittgenstein's mode of thought robs religious language of its unique significance. Because it removes the transcendent import of religious discourse, the language of "forms of life" can be seen as a sort of metalanguage in which we can state the final truth about other languages. If this charge were true, the language of forms of life would carry the same ultimacy for Wittgenstein as the language of science does for Frazer and his scientific soulmates.

This way of reading Wittgenstein does not do justice to his intentions. He rejects not only the idea that religious discourse is merely or primarily primitive science, but also the notion that there is any language other than the religious, including his own language of forms of life, that can adequately express religious claims. Wittgenstein's talk *about* religion is not a set of religious claims. Nor is it an attempt to offer an explanation of religious language or experience, as is the work of Frazer. Such an enterprise is explicitly rejected by Wittgenstein. Religious practices are not bad science, for the simple reason that they are not science at all. They constitute a characteristic and unique human response.[4] He remarks, "One could almost say that man is a ceremonial animal. That is, no doubt, partly wrong and partly nonsensical, but there is also something right about it" (*RFGB,* p. 129).

Wittgenstein has no sympathy with the typical philosophical move of subsuming one language, in this case religious language, under some other category. Religious languages and practices constitute a form life takes, and "one can only describe and say: this is what human life is like" (*RFGB,* p. 121). In this sense, then, religious practices can only be described; they cannot be reduced to or explained in other terms. What would "more fundamental" terms be like, in any case? The religious life is to be judged by history or science as little as they are to be judged by religion.[5] Each constitutes a different set of language-games, each must be judged by its own standards, and each is an expression of our "complicated form of life."

We must approach Wittgenstein's thoughts on these matters with great care if we are not to misunderstand them. When he attempts to see religious practices as a part of "this complicated form of life," he does not make a reductionist move. He is, in fact, making no move at all, except for disclaiming the idea that religious practices stand in need of explanation or justification. Those who see religious claims as primitive scientific views expect them to be displaced by the advance of science, leaving as their only task explaining how anyone could ever have believed such silly things. But we need to remember that in *Philosophical Investigations* Wittgenstein calls for doing away with all philosophical explanations and substituting descriptions for them (109). Religion seems problematic only if we treat it as a "theory" that might be true or false. Wittgenstein rejects all such accounts because they fail to see the unique character of the religious response. Again, "one can only describe and say: this is what human life is like."[6]

Religious claims must be understood and can be evaluated only from within their own tradition. Their meanings are determined by reference to their place within the relevant religious practices. ". . . I should like to say that in this case too [the case of religious language] the words you utter or what you think as you utter them are not what matters, so much as the difference they make at various points in your life. . . . Practice gives the words their sense" (*CV*, p. 85). There can be no doubt that religious practices make important differences in the lives of believers and that language has a central place within those practices. The words uttered in the context of sacred ceremonies have to be exactly right. Even the explanations of what happens in and through these rituals have to be couched in the correct language. Wittgenstein would have us turn to these practices and to the role language plays in them to discern the meaning of religious claims. He steadfastly rejects the assimilation of this function of language to any other of its functions or roles.

The factual-sounding declarative statements of religion may appear to be at odds with Wittgenstein's account. But this merely overlooks his famous distinction between surface grammar and depth grammar, which he thinks is often the source of philosophical confusion. Traditional philosophers regularly assimilate grammatically similar constructions to one another, with disastrous results. Supposing, for example, that the grammatical similarity of ritualistic sentences to historical statements is the key to understanding them has fueled repeated misunderstandings of religious language.

It is important to place Wittgenstein's remarks about religion in the proper context. He does not offer examinations or critiques of particular religious doctrines or of such controversies as that between Christians and Jews concerning the divinity of Jesus. These are differences that occur within religious life. They inform the lives of people of different religions, and they must be discussed and settled, if they can be settled at all, in the context of those living religions. Philosophers have no special competence to adjudicate matters of this sort. Nor is there a philosophical basis for assessing the religious response itself. In the first place, the religious life has no identifiable single essence. Moreover, there are no neutral terms in which such an evaluation could be mounted. With religion, as with mathematics and the values of the community, philosophy leaves everything as it is.

The utterances of religious believers contain, however, not only specifically religious statements, such as "Jesus is my personal savior" and "Praise be to God," but also sentences about the status of such claims. What might loosely be called a philosophy of religious language may tag along with the religious stance and gain uncritical acceptance, bringing religious assertions into apparent conflict with scientific or historical claims. So, for example, those who contend that we must accept either the Genesis account of creation or evolution, but not both, express not simply a religious commitment but also a philosophical view concerning the relation between religious and scientific claims.

Wittgenstein's response to such views is gratifyingly clear. He explicitly rejects the picture of religious assertions that brings them in conflict with science or history. In a passage written in 1937, he says:

> Christianity is not based on a historical truth; rather, it offers us a (historical) narrative and says: now believe. But not,

believe this narrative with the belief appropriate to a historical narrative, rather: believe, through thick and thin, which
you can do only as the result of a life. Here you have a narrative, don't take the same attitude to it as you take to other
historical narratives! Make a quite different place in your life
for it. (*CV*, p. 32)

Believing is different when it comes to religious claims than it is for
ordinary historical narratives. In his *Lectures and Conversations*,
Wittgenstein points out that people who have faith do not apply the
doubt that would be appropriate to historical propositions, especially propositions about a time long past. There is a natural skepticism
about ordinary historical claims for which we have very little independent evidence, especially if such claims are filled out with
exquisite details and removed to the distant past. Santayana makes
the same point in remarking that the very detail of the Gospels
should raise doubts in the ordinary person.[7] Although scholars such
as Ernest Renan and Albert Schweitzer have uniformly concluded
that the historical evidence for the Gospels is slim indeed, this seems
to make little difference to the faithful.[8]

That ordinary doubts about sacred claims tend not to dampen
faith suggests that religious belief is very different from beliefs of
other sorts. Just as sensible questions do not extinguish it, highly
confirmed empirical claims are inadequate to kindle it. Wittgenstein
says, "indubitability is not enough in this case. Even if there is as
much evidence as for Napoleon. Because the indubitability wouldn't
be enough to make me change my whole life." Religious faith is not
locatable on the usual continuum of beliefs between those open to
normal doubt and those that are indubitable, because it is not an
epistemic state. Nevertheless, the believer "has what you might call
an unshakable belief. It will show, not by reasoning or appeal to ordinary grounds for belief but rather by regulating [for] in all his life"
(*LC*, p. 54).

We must be careful not to confuse Wittgenstein's view with a familiar thesis. Priests, rabbis, and ministers often tell us that true religious
commitment is not a matter of mere intellectual assent; something

else must be grafted onto that acceptance—some change in our way of life. This position does not abjure the picture of religious faith that assimilates it to the intellectual assent model of belief. It just adds another element to intellectual assent. Faith is cognitive concurrence, along with some change in mode of life. The two are related in such a way that the former brings about the latter: we change our ways because we grasp certain important truths. For Wittgenstein, however, none of this will do. His position is more striking, as the following passage makes clear:

> Queer as it sounds: The historical accounts in the Gospels might, historically speaking, be demonstrably false and yet belief would lose nothing by this: *not* however, because it concerns 'universal truths of reason'! Rather because historical proof (the historical proof-game) is irrelevant to belief. This message (the Gospels) is seized on by men believingly (i.e. lovingly). *That* is the certainty characterizing this particular acceptance-as-true, not something *else*. (*CV*, p. 32)

The idea that the historical falsity of the Gospels would not weaken belief is truly radical. What does Wittgenstein mean? We must draw a distinction between the Jesus of the Gospels and any historical person or persons who may stand behind those texts.[9] Jesus is *present in* the Gospels and not merely described by them. When the believer comes into a transforming relation with the Jesus revealed in and through the Gospels, the historical background of the narrative recedes into irrelevance. Wittgenstein does not assert or deny the historical truth of the Gospels. He maintains that it has no bearing on the "particular acceptance-as-true" that constitutes faith. This provides a transformed understanding of religious believing. It conceives the relation of believers to what they believe as not intellectual assent, and it presents the content of their beliefs as not information of a historical or a metaphysical sort.

Something of what Wittgenstein is getting at is marked in ordinary language by the difference between "believing in" and "believing that." We believe *in* democracy, and we believe *that* Washington was the first president of the United States. In the former case, belief means devotion and commitment; in the latter, endorsement of a factual claim. Believing in the Christ of the Gospels and in the way of life embodied by him resembles the former and not the latter. Believers need have no opinion concerning the so-called historical Jesus. Wittgenstein says, "No *opinion* serves as the foundation for a religious symbol. And only an opinion can involve an error" (*RFGB*, p. 123).

While it is no doubt true that there are interesting and important connections between what I believe in and what I endorse as true, the two notions are quite distinct. Evidence, in the usual senses, is not relevant to believing in. In fact, one can and often does continue to believe in something, as Wittgenstein puts it, "through thick and thin," or against all odds and even in the face of evidence to the contrary. To believe in something does, of course, require an object or content, but that content is not normally some information or a set of putative facts. It is more likely to be persons or ideals or images of human possibility expressed in stories. Such ideals offer opportunities for personal transformation and altogether bypass or displace questions of historical truth.

This clearly is the notion of belief Wittgenstein has in mind when he remarks, "It strikes me that a religious belief could only be something like a passionate commitment to a system of reference. Hence, although it's *belief*, it's really a way of living, or a way of assessing life" (*CV*, p. 64, emphasis in the original). Wittgenstein's reason for calling special attention to the term "belief" is to counteract our inclination to treat it as "intellectual assent." To believe, in this sense, is not to accept certain propositions as true, but to be passionately committed to a way of living. There is, then, an internal or indissoluble connection between one's religious beliefs and one's way of life.[10] This seems to be of overriding importance for Wittgenstein. Throughout his discussions, he focuses over and over again on the role religious beliefs play in the conduct of our lives. This means that our relation to religious commitments is not epistemic but practical. In the face of what is possibly a total lack of evidence, we are still willing to risk everything (*LC*, p. 54). His talk of "passionate commitment to a system of reference" underscores that we are prepared to take such beliefs as the standards by which to shape our lives. There is no logical gap between acting and believing in this context. To believe passionately in democracy is to work to bring it about or to sustain it, and to assess the legitimacy of governments using it as the standard. Similarly, to believe passionately in Jesus as one's savior is to be willing to follow his example and to assess the value of actions by using his commandments as the final standard.

The cognitivist theory of faith treats this aspect of religious believing as an addendum to its "accepting-as-true" approach. For Wittgenstein, on the other hand, "believing means submitting to an authority." To submit to an authority is to accept its dictates, be they those of an individual (such as Jesus Christ) or of an ideal (such as democracy) as the final legitimate ground for action or opinion. If I have submitted to an authority, then I cannot "reserve the right to an independent judgment." As Wittgenstein says, "Having once submitted, you can't then, without rebelling against it, first call it in question and then once again find it acceptable" (CV, p. 45). On what grounds could an independent judgment be made? Any grounds that might lead to different actions or opinions would be irrelevant or at most evil, not erroneous.

Wittgenstein offers us three interrelated points. First, having faith or endorsing religious claims is not intellectual assent in the light of evidence or supported by an intuitive or extrarational faculty. Instead it is a passionate commitment. Second, faith does not put us in relation to a proposition that conveys information. Rather it commits us passionately to an authority as determinative for our lives. Finally, this authority does not derive its right to command from some further authority (in which case it would be possible to call it into question without "rebelling against it"). We cannot appeal to the authority of reason, for example, or to prudence to justify or to defend our religious commitments. Religious language presents believers with the authoritative as immediate and definitive for their lives.

To use familiar terminology, religious talk is a very different language-game from those in which the point is to state facts, such as the language-games of history and physics. In the *Tractatus*

Logico-Philosophicus, Wittgenstein says, "The general form of a proposition is: This is how things stand" (4.5). That is, language has a single essence, which is to convey information or to picture facts. Since religious language does not do that, on Wittgenstein's early view it was literally nonsensical. He thought that what such language attempts to say is beyond saying. In the later work, however, Wittgenstein rejects the ideas that language has an essence and that we can specify a priori what can and what cannot be said. We must look and see what different language-games can and what they cannot do. This means that the measure of sense is the actual use of language. And we determine that by looking not at what information is conveyed, but at what role the language plays in the lives of the people who use it. Since the language of religion has a significant place in many lives, it can not be dismissed as meaningless or assimilated to some ideal notion sense or language.

A personal question may emerge from this discussion. Where is Wittgenstein in all this, that is, what is his relation to religious discourse? Clearly in his philosophical reflections he is not personally within any religious tradition. In fact, he announces that he is not a religious man.[11] Both he and Santayana are spectators of the scene— a scene they attempt to locate in the realm of human life and to describe. Wittgenstein considers it enough if he can achieve a certain clarity of conception. He expresses deep respect for the many forms of religious commitment, but they appear to him mainly as objects to be viewed and liberated from the unwelcome interference of philosophy. In the final analysis, his is a contemplative stance that does not favor engagement. Once he gains a "perspicuous representation," he is satisfied to leave everything as it is. Even such clarity is not of permanent importance for, as he says in *Culture and Value,* "At present we are combating a trend. But this trend will die out, superseded by others and then the way we are arguing against it will no longer be understood; people will not see why all this needed saying" (p. 43).

He views even his own work as only of passing value. This perspective locates him outside of his own project. The ultimate spectatorial quality of his work and stance, along with his readiness to accept the forms human life takes, suggests a distant, transcendent perspective. Looked at from without, the multiplicity of religious commitments can all be seen as wonderful; each can be appreciated for its uniqueness and integrity once all claims to theory and truth have been set aside. Wittgenstein's concern is to free religious people from the unjustified demands of philosophy and thereby to return them to the immediacy of their practice. That he does not share that practice is a matter of personal sensibility, not philosophical commitment.[12]

Santayana's relation to religion is also complex and personal. His father was a freethinker, but his beloved sister, Susanna, was a deeply believing Catholic. He was attracted by the rich symbolism of Christianity, even though he never found its authority adequate to compel belief. Instead, from his early *Interpretations of Poetry and Religion* to *The Idea of Christ in the Gospels,* written late in life,[13] he engaged in the loving study of religions and in the attempt to understand their power.

On occasion he showed impatience with the claims of religious people. For example, he refers to the discussion of two seminarians in the gardens of Seville about the perfection of angels as "dreaming in words" (*SAF,* p. 7). But for the most part, he viewed religion as a highway by which we may approach the deeper yearnings of the human heart. The descriptive content of Christianity is not to be taken literally: even though claims about heaven and hell, for instance, look as though they refer to geographical regions, we miss the point if we look for these places in the empirical world. Instead they need to be seen as revealing some deep moral insight about the human condition. We thus find him in complete agreement with Wittgenstein that the role of religious discourse is not to convey factual information but to articulate life-transforming ideals.

This point is made well in the preface of his first book on religion:

> Religious doctrines would do well to withdraw their pretension to be dealing with matters of fact. That pretension is not only the source of the conflicts of religion with science and of the vain and bitter controversies of sects; it is also the cause

of the impurity and incoherence of religion in the soul, when
it seeks its sanctions in the sphere of reality, and forgets that
its proper concern is to express the ideal. (*IPR*, p. v)

The function of the symbolism of religion is not to give us additional
insight into the structure of the world but to focus the ideals by
which life is enriched and fulfilled.

Santayana's view that religious statements are symbolic is complicated by the fact that, strictly, he does not think there is any literal
knowledge at all. The chance that the essences rising to consciousness through the operation of our senses are identical to those embodied in the material world is slim at best. The ultimate units of
matter, he keeps repeating, are out of scale with our senses. "The
garment of appearance must always fit [matter] loosely and drape it
in alien folds, because appearance is essentially an adaptation of
facts to the scale and faculty of the observer" (*RB*, p. xii). For this
reason, we must be satisfied with appropriate symbolism even in our
perceptual life. Knowledge itself is nothing but empirical confidence
in the existence of a substantial and independent world, mediated by
essences that serve as signs of what surrounds us.

Viewing all cognitive activity as symbolic may appear to reinsti-
tute the rivalry between science and religion. It might be thought that
if they do not compete for the best factual account of the origin of
the world and of humans in it, they vie in trying to provide the best
symbolism for expressing truths. And this indeed is what Santayana
suggests here and there. He says, for example, that calling the moon
a "virgin goddess" and "an extinct and opaque spheroidal satellite
of the earth" are alternative descriptions of it, equally symbolic but
differentially useful (*SAF*, pp. 176–77).

Nevertheless this is not his final and considered opinion.
Although perception and the findings of science are couched in
essences, their function is to lay bare "the dynamic relations of
events." We try to keep them "closer to animal faith, and freer from
pictorial elements" than other forms of symbolism (*SAF*, p. 178).
They constitute a part of the response of the psyche to the pressure
of external events. The response is under the constant control of

outer circumstance, recording for us the alignment and realignments of the material world.

The symbolism of religion, by contrast, is devoted largely to expressing the internal constitution, the values, and the predicaments of the psyche. Though religious statements are often conveyed in declarative sentences, Santayana agrees with Wittgenstein that they do not describe anything. They are neither theories that constitute a primitive science nor cognitive attempts to give a factual account of the nature or origin of the world. To say that they express the values and predicaments of the psyche is to call attention to their function of distilling and publicizing our commitments. Such expressions are both useful and necessary for the guidance of life.

Santayana's view is remarkably similar to Wittgenstein's on this point. The function of religious discourse is not to convey information that may be true or false or to state theories that require intellectual assent. It is, rather, to express passionate commitments to structuring values. Such a religious articulation of the good enables the soul to sing: in displaying what it believes in, it can at once bring itself in closer conformity to it.

This is the reason why Santayana associates religion with poetry. Both are products of the human imagination, if this faculty is seen as a vital and constructive element of human life. Both offer visions of the ideal, of what would truly satisfy. The fundamental difference between them is that religion aims at guiding the course of existence: "poetry is called religion when it intervenes in life." Santayana is even more direct and specific at a later point in the same work, saying that "religion is poetry become the guide of life." When the poet expresses "the true visions of his people and of his soul, his poetry is the consecration of his deepest convictions, and contains the whole truth of his religion" (*IPR*, pp. 289, 290).

So the ultimate thrust of religious belief is to transform the life of the believer. Such transformation is impossible on the basis of intellectual assent or insight. A vital commitment is needed, and it can be attained only if the ideal articulated is native to the psyche. Ideals hold authority because they capture the fundamental impulses of the organism and mobilize it into action. The activities ignited consume, even while they fulfill and complete, the entire life of the person. This is living at white heat, as Santayana speaks of it, or with a passion that engulfs and satisfies the soul.

The immediate authority Wittgenstein finds in religious language is thus also fully recognized by Santayana. As usual, however, Santayana goes a step further than Wittgenstein in trying to understand the phenomenon. He thinks its ground lies in the perfect correspondence between the nature of the psyche and the purposes that engage it. The motto of *The Life of Reason* is that everything natural has an ideal completion, and everything ideal a natural ground. The ideals religions articulate constitute extensions and expressions of natural life; their authority derives not from any external source, but from the internal impulses of the organism.

This analysis brings the differences between the symbolism of perception and science, on the one hand, and the symbolism of religion, on the other, into sharper relief. The former, as we said, is under the perpetual control of external facts; its aim is to provide a lean and functionally accurate account of the swirl of matter around us. The latter is an attempt to give voice to the inner self, not by describing or understanding it but by identifying its ideals, clarifying its attachments, and living by its commands. It is, in brief, an attempt at self-expression that is at once the self-realization of our inner nature or psyche. The religious form of such self-realization is free of the philosophical demand for rational self-knowledge. It has its own integrity and operates by a sort of instinctive self-recognition, feeling its way among values and ideals until it finds something it can experience as authoritative and yet comfortable.

As the "self-maintaining and reproducing pattern or structure of an organism" (RB, p. 569), the psyche is an organ of vegetation and choice, sustaining our lives by its continuous but highly selective activity. This selectivity or animal preference is, for Santayana, the foundation of good and evil. When its selections are apt, the goods the psyche embraces truly satisfy it; when they are not, its life is unhappy or short. The selections and their consequences affect spirit when they rise to consciousness as felt fulfillments or dissatisfactions.

"Spirit" is Santayana's term for the light of awareness or "the total *inner* difference between being awake or asleep, alive or dead" (*RB,* p. 572). Although consciousness originates in and is sustained by the physical organism, its nature is remarkably different from that of the psyche. The difference also has its source in the psyche, which aims its activities in two different directions. The two lines of activity or self-expression create two different sorts of religion. The first is a religion of "piety toward the source" (*RR,* p. 125), the second an ultimate or spiritual religion.

Struggling in an alien world or in one at best indifferent to its needs, the psyche develops respect for the force that governs its fortunes. It learns to venerate matter, whose bounty provides it with the conditions of its flourishing. In the language of Christianity, this is gratitude to the Father to whom the faithful pray for their daily bread. Without the benevolence of this boundless force, life could not have started and could not now be sustained. Service and supplication are appropriate to this God, the Lord and giver of life, who holds us in his hands and whose ire could destroy the individual and even the race. At harvest and at moments of victory, this is the God we praise as God Almighty, thanking him for "our creation, preservation, and all the blessings of this life."

The danger of this form of religion is that it can easily turn into superstition. A shrewd bargain of money for divine favor can take the place of thankfulness, and prayer can become a way of trying to direct the will of God. If we think that gifts to the gods or religious rites are substitutes for the laborious transformation of nature, we drift in the direction of magic and feel tempted to believe that faith is a rival, and more effective, method of thriving than science and rational husbandry.

Ultimate religion is the spirituality of which Santayana speaks at length, especially in his later works. Even nonhuman animals show a fascination with the appearance of things; dogs seem to enjoy the play of flames in the fire as much as humans do. With us, attention to the immediate has grown from a satisfying diversion to a powerful and recurrent tendency. When we are absorbed in the moment, concern about ambient forces recedes, and we are able to enjoy essences for their own sake. The dance of light on the water, distant hills clad in snow, and the silk of a baby's skin capture us for an eternal second and set us free from stress and fear.

Such momentary escape from the practical teaches us to view everything as God would see it. The vision misses nothing of the complexity of the world, but its distance makes it cool. Partiality and animal heat are abandoned, and everything becomes crisp, clear, and changelessly itself. Pure spirit views the involutions of history with the detachment of a spectator at an infinite remove, converting actual events into "chronicles of ancient wars" (*SAF,* p. 125). The result is a celebration of consciousness, of the Holy Spirit in religious language,[14] that spreads joy throughout life. This relegates selectivity to irrelevance: every essence presented is enjoyed in a wonderful drunkenness with being.

This ultimate religion is closer to what flourishes in India than to what is everyday in the West. Yet there are traces of it in primitive religion, and the mystical, joyous, and celebratory reaches of the Judeo-Christian tradition give ample insight into its nature. It is a religion without explicit theology, readily acknowledging that it needs no theory and hence offering no descriptions of fact. It provides instead the privileges of spectatorship, of taking joy in seeing the contest from a great distance or under the form of eternity. Though they were not religious men, Santayana and Wittgenstein shared the attitudes, the insights, and the pleasures of this religion of the mind.

Chapter 6

CONCLUSION

We have shown pervasive and persuasive similarities between the thought of Wittgenstein and that of Santayana. They differ, to be sure, on a number of issues, and we have no desire to obscure those important divergences. But the resemblances are striking, and only the current fragmented state of philosophy, in which specialization in analytic, Continental, or American problems and texts largely excludes appreciation of the others, can explain the fact that they have gone unrecognized.

Despite the convergences, however, Santayana's and Wittgenstein's ideas seem very different even to the careful observer. What accounts for this feeling of unlikeness in the teeth of substantial similarity? The contrast between their styles of writing and reflection must hold at least a part of the key. In places *Philosophical Investigations* reads like a string of notes in need of being worked into a good first draft.[1] Santayana, on the other hand, wrote drafts even of his letters and published only what he thought was elegantly lucid. Wittgenstein's tortured struggles with philosophical problems stand at the opposite extreme from Santayana's polished expression of his distilled views. The former seems to provide a glimpse of the ambiguities and reversals of the process of thinking; the latter shows only its perfectly honed products. Wittgenstein is all caution and apparent indecision; Santayana never seems to lose direction or to hesitate.

Important as this variance of style may be, it is not the only, or perhaps even the major, factor in creating the look of difference. The two thinkers differ in philosophical idiom, in the language and conceptual framework in which they choose to express their views.

Wittgenstein continually turns our attention to language—to what we say—while Santayana speaks of things, actions, and relationships. This seems to exaggerate their disagreements at least partly because the variance between the formal and the material modes of language appears at first sight to be vast. Yet the disparity between these two ways of communicating is not so great as to make it impossible to use them to express closely related points.

Santayana's chosen idiom is the language of the grand tradition of philosophy that reaches back through medieval logic to Aristotle and Plato. The use of such terms as substance, essence, matter, and spirit naturally inclines him to ontology. The ontological discourse, in turn, suggests that his primary aim is to give an inventory of the sorts of beings of which the world consists. This may prompt us to assimilate him to thinkers such as Descartes, Spinoza, and Leibniz, many of whose disagreements focused on the types and the number of substances constituting the cosmos. Those who yield to this temptation see Santayana as a faint echo of old ways of philosophizing, a halfhearted accountant checking the balance sheets of the universe. The result is the seriously mistaken supposition that Santayana is a system builder after the systems have failed, an atavistic anomaly in contemporary thought.

People who take this view refuse to accept Santayana's own account of his intentions. He announces early and clearly that his thought constitutes "no system of the universe." It is an elaboration of "the workaday opinions of mankind," focused on getting clear about "the chief issue, the relation of man and his spirit to the universe." The ontology is thus in the service of what might be described as broadly moral purposes. It is, moreover, thoroughly ironic in its outcomes. Universals in the Platonic tradition, for example, typically serve as objects of knowledge and standards of proper function. By recognizing an infinity of such essences, Santayana undercuts their normal and expected role; as objects of immediate acquaintance they cannot be *known* and their prolix specificity makes them unfit to be compelling criteria of anything (*SAF,* pp. vi, v, viii).

Santayana's accounts of the other realms are bathed in similar irony. Matter is supposed to be the ultimate explanatory principle of

Conclusion

existence, but its inner nature is unintelligible. Truth is the silent, unerasable witness of everything that happens, the objective record of the march of facts. Yet it includes every perspective any mind takes on any fact and thereby erases the difference between true and false perception or belief. Spirit remains irreducible to any bodily part or physical behavior, extending its influence to every area of value and human concern. Nevertheless consciousness is incapable of exerting power over events and must, in its impotence, turn to the silent enjoyment of eternal forms.

The point of Santayana's ontological idiom, therefore, is very different from the use earlier thinkers made of similar categories. These traditional notions enable him to systematize his reflections. But, in the process, they also give him an opportunity to take an ironic glance at the history of philosophy, smiling at the earnest literalness with which such notions have been taken. For him, they are only symbols to explicate our modes of action and to mark interesting or important aspects of the human experience. We cannot understand the deeply modern, even postmodern, stance of Santayana without due appreciation of his powerful affirmation of the legitimacy of what we do, his mockery of self-satisfied philosophers, and his ambivalence about the enterprise of understanding, let alone criticizing, all of human life. The significance of Santayana's ontology is not in the sorts of being it distinguishes, but in the insights it gives into the structures and operations of the human world.

The point of Wittgenstein's chosen idiom can also be seriously misunderstood. His orientation can be seen to have turned from world to word, from the effort to understand the structure of the universe in his earlier work to the attempt to clear up linguistic confusions in the later. But this perspective on his thought is misleading. He does indeed take language as the primary subject matter of his thinking; in doing so he presents philosophical problems in the fashion current in his intellectual milieu. But whatever may be true of other philosophers in his tradition, "turning to the word" does not make Wittgenstein face away from the world. One might argue that, on the contrary, only this revolution permits the real world to gain a place in his thinking.

The "world" of Wittgenstein's early work, the structured totality of facts, is a philosopher's world, created by an illusory problematic. Only his disillusionment with the ideas of the *Tractatus* and his related rejection of an ideal language capable of capturing the crystalline structure of the world enabled him to see the impenetrable complexities of what surrounds us. Accordingly, when the later Wittgenstein speaks of language, he locates it within the matrix of human practices in a universe of contingencies on whose general structure it is idle for us to reflect. As we noted before, he says that to imagine a language is to imagine a form of life.[2]

But Wittgenstein does not stop there. Our actions and broader practices occur in a context; they require and appropriate the natural and the social world in which they come to fruition or fail. Human forms of life, including the languages we use to communicate with one another, exist among "facts of nature" and within "natural history" and so presuppose the natural world. By turning to the word, Wittgenstein at once turns to the world and explores the significance of language as a tool of human action within that world.

Some philosophers interpret Wittgenstein as a sort of linguistic idealist, holding that we are sealed up in communicative practices we can never escape.[3] But such a reading utterly ignores the fact that he locates language within this larger milieu. The commitment to the living context is precisely what turns him *away* from language in the narrow sense and turns him *to* the world. The grand philosophical tradition's tendency to overlook the situated, that is, the worldly, character of our practices is the primary reason for its continued call for foundations or self-justifying justifications. By contrast, Wittgenstein gives due acknowledgment to the reality that surrounds us and thereby, ironically perhaps, acquires the right to charge that tradition with not taking the world seriously enough.

So, although it is true that Wittgenstein makes language the focus of his philosophical reflections, this does not, except in relatively superficial terms of idiom, put him at odds with Santayana. The same is true of the anti-ontological bent of Wittgenstein's thought. As we have just noted, Santayana's ontological categories systematically undercut the traditional philosophical understanding of the ontological

Conclusion

project. This does not, of course, imply that we are to understand his "realms of being" in merely negative terms. On the contrary, in what follows we will explore in detail Santayana's positive ontological claims and their relation to Wittgenstein's views. The relevant point here is that a central purpose of his ironic ontology is to let the air out of the grand metaphysical systems of the past. The sensibilities that underlie this self-displacing ontology are the same that motivate Wittgenstein's anti-ontological stance.

In his early work, Wittgenstein set about seeing the world as a completed totality and discovered or at least exhibited that the attempt to carry out such a project reduces itself to silence.[4] In a passage of the preface to *Philosophical Investigations* deserving of more attention than it has received, Wittgenstein remarks that that work "could be seen in the right light only by contrast with and against the background of my old way of thinking" (vii). His early work, with its distinctions between "objects and facts" and between "language and world," represents Wittgenstein's attempt to think through the ontological project. What enables us to see the methods of the *Philosophical Investigations* in a new light is the failure of that project, that is, its self-imploding reduction to silence.

In his later work, Wittgenstein carefully avoids all attempts to enter into the project of traditional ontology. He shows over and over again that, if we begin where we live, that is, in our situated practices, uncontextualized questions of vast generality cannot legitimately arise. For Wittgenstein, ontology is impossible simply because we cannot attain the perspective necessary to take an objective inventory of all there is. Surprisingly and clearly, he is in complete agreement with Santayana on this point. Only their approaches differ: Wittgenstein altogether refuses to take up ontology, while Santayana displaces it by means of an "ontology" that undercuts its own objectivity.[5]

This deep similarity hiding behind superficial difference is analogous to what we discovered with regard to the problem of knowledge. There we saw that Santayana thinks the resolute attempt to take the skeptic seriously reduces the philosopher to ignorant silence, while Wittgenstein believes that even the attempt to get the skeptical enterprise started misconceives the nature and status of our cognitive practices. Their substantive views are identical, though Santayana reaches his by fighting his way through the entire skeptical reduction, while Wittgenstein refuses even to engage in the project. The former shows the bankruptcy of the enterprise, the latter its illegitimacy. Throughout it all, the differences in strategy guise an identity of ultimate belief.

In just this way, their apparently divergent attitudes to ontology are tactical only. Both reject the possibility of taking inventory of the realities that populate the world. Wittgenstein does so by refusing to engage in the enterprise altogether, while Santayana shows that it lacks universal validity, amounting to no more than a single individual clearing "the windows of his soul" (*SAF,* pp. vi–vii). Here again, their substantive positions are identical, even though the roads that take them there wind through different parts of the country.

The full extent of their agreement is best revealed by reflection on the aspects of our experience of the world that Santayana wants to stress in his four realms of being. Throughout, the language of ontology is meant not to reveal hidden realities or to bear "tidings from a Spirit-World" (*RB,* p. 549). Rather it prefigures or symbolically indicates certain pervasive features of experienced reality. Even if their rhetoric sometimes belies their acts, the behavior of human beings takes these characteristics fully into account. Santayana and Wittgenstein agree that philosophers would be well advised to heed the wisdom embodied in our activities and to bring their reflections in line with our practices.

To this point, our discussion of matters relating to ontology has remained at a relatively abstract level. To make good our case for substantial agreement between our two thinkers requires a more detailed discussion of Santayana's realms of being in relation to Wittgenstein's views than we have provided so far. Clearly neither adopts the traditional ontological project, so we can safely say that they are in agreement on the negative side. Yet one could argue that such concurrence is not unusual in the twentieth century even among thinkers who are of one mind on little else. We must now show,

Conclusion

therefore, that there are also central positive points of correspondence in their views.

One cannot deny that Santayana makes liberal use of ontological language, while Wittgenstein not only does not but actually argues against its use. This difference is real and represents a fundamental divergence in philosophical attitudes between the two. Yet we maintain that a close examination of the role ontological distinctions play in Santayana—of what he does with these categories in developing his philosophical ideas—displays that many of the differences are only apparent. We shall try to show that although Santayana's and Wittgenstein's resources, tools, and strategies are different, the philosophical goals they wish to achieve by means of them are remarkably similar. To demonstrate this, we will review Santayana's realms of being and discuss their functions in his philosophy. We shall then compare the points they help Santayana make with Wittgenstein's considered opinions.

When Santayana speaks about realms of being, he does not mean cosmological regions or even separate sorts of existents. They are, he says, "not parts of the cosmos, nor one great cosmos together," being instead significant distinctions worth making in the process of pursuing the primary task of philosophy, which is the promotion of clear vision in the service of better life. This underscores that Santayana does not attempt to achieve the sort of "view from nowhere" that has been the traditional goal of the ontological project. He states at the outset that the transcendence required for metaphysics of the classical sort is beyond our capacity. There is, moreover, little objective and nothing compulsory about Santayana's distinctions. He invites anybody dissatisfied with them to do better: "Let him clean better, if he can, the windows of his soul, that the variety and beauty of the prospect may spread more brightly before him" (*SAF,* p. vi).

Santayana distinguishes four realms of being: essence, matter, truth, and spirit. When he speaks of an infinity of essences, he does not mean that this multitude actually exists. To the contrary, the hallmark of essences is that the being appropriate to them is not existence. If we distinguish the many meanings of the word "is"

(Santayana distinguishes seven),[6] essences *are* only in the sense in which "is" indicates self-identity. Everything that can exist or that anyone can think of—and that means every being, quality, and relation—is a self-identical essence. That there are infinities of them is clear if we reflect even for a moment on the number of numbers, each of which is an essence, self-identically and timelessly itself.

At one point, Santayana speaks of essences as the "costumes" existence wears.[7] This is both accurate and misleading: accurate because all the features of existence are essences, misleading because there are many essences that can be only thought of and never embodied in the world. Essences enjoy some of the characteristics normally attributed to forms or universals. But Santayana radicalizes the idea of form in a way that takes away the moral and ontological prerogatives with which philosophers normally endow it.

If every quality and relation is an essence, forms can range from the vastly general to the minutely specific. This guarantees that even fully determinate relations are universals, as are the complexes of forms that define existing individuals. Accordingly, in good Platonic fashion, there is a form of humanity, but also a form for every existing and even possible person. And since we change in the course of time, there is a different form that defines us with each turn in our fortunes.

Forms themselves do not change, but they make it possible for us to understand change as the exchange of the qualities and relations of existing things. The infinity, eternity, and determinateness of universals render the realm of essence a democracy: none of its members has moral prerogatives, and none is more real than any other. We might think of them simply as a cornucopia of objects for attention, of whose reality we do not need to be convinced the moment we pay them heed.

The realm of essence is Santayana's symbolic means of conveying the pluralism of structures. Essences are infinitely numerous and include forms of every sort and every complexity. Although Santayana speaks on occasion of the single, staggeringly complicated form that is the essence of the history of the universe, he thinks that such totalizing structures are at home only in the dialectical speculations of philosophers. In reality every existing thing embodies an indefinitely large number of forms, some easily discerned and others emerging only as we consider objects in their interrelations. This implies the exact opposite of what one would expect in a philosophy that uses the notion of essence: nothing in the world has a single, defining, developmentally time-spanning essence. The vast multiplicity of forms makes it impossible to hold that any item is defined by a solitary form and that reality at large has a single logical structure.

The pluralism of structures is only a short step away from the pluralism of descriptions and redescriptions. Santayana's commitment to a multitude of forms is the equivalent of Wittgenstein's view of the multiplicity of language-games. This open-ended diversity of communicative structures undercuts the attempt to take any particular language as privileged in a final or absolute way. Each is simply a different discourse that may serve certain purposes better than other languages do. Beyond that, no language can claim special authority. Thus there is no single description that can give us the "essence" of a thing and no language-game that can provide a final account of "reality." In fact, we are not limited even to the existing multiplicity of language-games, for we can always create new games by inventing "fictitious natural history." (*PI*, part 2, 230) The play of varied and alternative language-games displaces or breaks the hold of the idea of single essential descriptions.

Admittedly the term "essence" carries negative connotations for Wittgenstein. But that is easily explained by the fact that it is tied for him to its traditional meaning, a meaning Santayana's view of the realm of essence is meant to undercut. The important similarity this verbal difference obscures is that commitment to the infinity of essences and demonstration of the indefinite multiplicity of language-games are both strategies for getting out of the blind alley of essentialism.

Santayana's view of essence is designed to remind us, moreover, that the necessary has only a contingent application to life. Since logical necessity is internal to essence, it does not carry through to guide or demand the instantiation of any essence in the world. There is neither a living purpose that imposes necessity on existence nor a self-actualizing necessary structure to reality. Leibniz was mistaken in thinking that possibles clamor for actuality, that the good can charm its way into reality, and that essence and existence meet in an infinite, necessary Being. Since implications in the realm of essence run in every direction, even our ordinary inferences involve contingent selectivity. We are not compelled to select any one essence to characterize a situation; there are always others. The essence we select, moreover, does not compel inferential movement. As a result, the success of inference is never a purely logical question.

Wittgenstein's discussion of language also confirms this point. All necessity is internal to the language-games we play, having its source in the rules of the game. In *Remarks on the Foundations of Mathematics,* Wittgenstein considers the "inexorability with which two follows from one and three two" and says, "But presumably this means: follows in the series of cardinal numbers." That is the game being played, and those are the rules of the game. There is no more to necessity than that. Counting, of course, is not to be taken as a mere pastime. It has a certain pervasive place in our activities, and "The *truth* is that counting has proved to pay" (p. 37). We see the contingency in recognizing that it might not have turned out that way. For our language-games are situated in a larger natural and social context, where we can speak only of possible causes and hypotheses, not of logical necessity.[8] Necessity has its home within language-games, and these exist in a wider world of contingency. Santayana and Wittgenstein both have a keen sense of the pervasive character of this encompassing contingency.

The realm of essence encompasses every quality, relation, and structure, and each of its elements is recognizably different from every other. It includes even the square circle, which, Santayana says, is a term in comic discourse.[9] This realm constitutes, therefore, the ultimate counter to reductionism of any sort. Each essence is irreducibly different from every other. One and one *make* two, without becoming identical with it. Whatever is good may also be desired or of interest to a living creature, but being good is not the same as being desired or being the object of someone's interest. A person is not a collection of social roles, and mind cannot be reduced to brain processes.

Conclusion

In ordinary life, we rush to treat essences as signs of the world around us, impoverishing experience by overlooking their intrinsic characters. When philosophers fail to respect difference, they face a special loss: the urge to make headway with their theories seduces them to affirm hasty identities. The corrective is to provide sensitive descriptions capable of focusing our minds on the character of the essence before us, an activity Santayana embraces again and again.

Wittgenstein stresses the significance of difference no less. His insistence on it is at the very center of his discussion of family resemblances. He argues that our use of general terms need not be backed by the presence of a common property in all the individuals to which it applies. There may instead be an overlapping network of similarities and differences. Our use of the *same term* may blind us to differences. We say that there must be something in common, but Wittgenstein reminds us to "look and see." He contends, moreover, that the assimilation of the use of a term in one context to its use in another creates a great deal of philosophical confusion. He thinks this error important enough to highlight it at the beginning of *Philosophical Investigations* when he discusses the assimilation of all words to names.

Throughout his later work, Wittgenstein reminds us of the multiplicity of language-games. Each has its own integrity that keeps it different from all others. None can be reduced to another. So, as we have seen, the language of religion is not the language of science. Our talk about value is not to be analyzed or defined in terms of some other way of talking. Description, he thinks, must replace attempts to explain or to define. The similarity to Santayana is, once again, remarkable.

Admittedly Santayana makes the point in the language of essences and Wittgenstein in terms of language-games. But this is only the difference of idiom we noted before, guising substantial agreement. One might also suppose that the contrast between Wittgenstein's jumbled, open-ended multiplicity of language-games and the completed infinity of Santayana's realm of essence makes the two philosophers part company. But the infinity of the realm of essence renders it a wilderness, and its totality is but an imaginative projection. It is, in other words, only as orderly as our exploration of it, which is open-ended and full of jumbled starts and reversals.

The realm of essence is a frozen world in the sense that such forms of determinateness, being unchanging, can account neither for change nor for their own embodiment. What makes for existence, in the proper sense of things standing in external relations to one another, is the restless and largely unintelligible force Santayana calls "matter." Since forms lack dynamism and stand only in the internal relations of identity and difference, they cannot bring themselves into being. Matter, on the other hand, is difficult to conceptualize: each time we find some form that seems to serve well as the essence of existence, we realize that *as form* it could never do the job of selection reserved for matter. The physical dynamism of matter exceeds any form in terms of which we may try to understand it: that anything exists at all and this thing here are, in the end, past explanation.

Speaking in the anthropomorphizing language of what he calls literary psychology, Santayana says that matter wrests essences from their peaceful eternity and thrusts them in the swirling world of existence. It is thus an "insane emphasis" and a "whirlwind," suggesting that our primary relation to it is physical, not intellectual. We cannot understand it, yet ride its cycles and rhythms until we wear out or some cataclysm buries our small part of the world. Matter has neither purpose nor intelligence. Its indifference to our existence denies us the happy illusion that we are the favored children of creation. To be sure, it provides sufficient order for us to exist. But that order is accidental and evanescent, allowing us only partial and tenuous control over the course of our lives.

Although Wittgenstein does not thematize the tenuousness of human projects in anything like Santayana's ontological terms, its recognition, as we have seen, is at the center of his thinking. Discussions of Wittgenstein often overlook that he locates human activities, including language, in a world that conditions them. Our use of language and of the particular language we speak is, for him, a function of facts about ourselves and our world that might well have been different. He often refers to our "natural history" and says that though he is not doing natural science, he must take account of the fact that "Our interest certainly includes the correspondence between concepts and very general facts of nature" (*PI*, 415; part 2, 230). We find ourselves in a world not of our own making, a world in which our prosperity is not guaranteed. Wittgenstein wonders,

> would it be unthinkable that I should stay in the saddle however much the facts bucked?
>
> Certain events would put me into a position in which I could not go on with the old language-game any further. In which I was torn away from the *sureness* of the game.
>
> Indeed, doesn't it seem obvious that the possibility of a language-game is conditioned by certain facts? (*OC*, 616–17)

This is a poignant reminder that our language, our thoughts, and our actions all occur at the sufferance of greater forces. They exist in a world that, as it happens, "behaves kindly" but that gives no guaranty that we will always "stay in the saddle."

There is an even deeper point Santayana wishes to convey by means of the symbol of matter. Since forms are the immediate objects present to intuition, all knowledge occurs through their mediation. The essence intuited need not be identical with the one embodied in the world so long as there is an appropriate symbolic connection between them. But such relations always involve essences serving as signs of essences. This is not how things stand with matter, which, Santayana thinks, is the formless other of essence. To know it, we must use an essence as symbol, yet no essence can capture such structureless dynamism. At the same time, even referring to matter as a structureless dynamism utilizes essences to convey the nature of something that has no nature.

The ensuing paradox, consisting of the need to understand that which passes all understanding or the attempt to explicate an inexplicable mystery, reduces or perhaps elevates Santayana's language to poetry. The word "matter" is, when all is said and done, a poetic term without literal significance, merely gesturing toward that which lies at the limit of all meaning. Santayana is thus a materialist in the time-honored sense of believing that a philosophy that treats form as an all-encompassing and adequate category cannot be complete. Such a materialism places forms and meanings in a broader field of unintelligibility. To put it in the way postmodern thinkers do, Santayana shows how our attempt to understand everything is excessive. Such an effort leads past essences to unintelligible matter, revealing that the very enterprise of intellectual grasp presupposes something that exceeds it.

This remarkable anticipation of postmodern insights brings Santayana close to Wittgenstein as well. Although his language is different, Wittgenstein clearly agrees with the fundamental point. Throughout the *Philosophical Investigations,* he argues that meaning is a function of the language-games in which terms have their proper use. Within language-games, general questions of legitimacy cannot be raised because, if challenged, we can always say that this is just the way the game is played. Beyond established language-games, once again, no questions of legitimacy can arise, though for another reason: there we have no linguistic practices that would justify or forbid any query or answer.

Such relativizing of meaning to language-games bears fruit in two areas of concern. It validates our established linguistic practices, and it stops worthless questioning beyond them. In this way, Wittgenstein is committed to understand meaning as circumscribed by a larger field of nonmeaning and intelligible discourse as encircled by a world of facts. He makes the point best when he discusses what is involved in explaining things. He notes that, just as there is always a last house on the street, there must also be a last explanation, beyond which we find only stretches of brute fact or unexplained reality.[10]

Santayana believes that truth, or what others have called fact, is an objective, unchangeable reality. As such, it is a portion of the realm of essence. In fact, he argues that the realm of truth is simply that segment of the realm of essence that has been, is being, or will ever be actualized in the real world. His claim that truth is "the standard comprehensive description" of a fact is misleading if not properly understood (*SAF,* pp. 266ff). By "description" he does not mean to imply that human activity need be involved; in fact, all that is needed is that matter selectively and successively embody some essences. That the truth is a standard suggests that we can fall short of capturing it in our accounts—a well known fact about human beings. It is comprehensive, moreover, in that elements of it have no moral or other prerogatives—any and every essence embodied, no matter how low or trivial, is a part of it.

On this view, truth appears to be objective and independent of human opinion. It is the full and eternal record of the history of the world in all its detailed misery and glory. To use a helpful historical analogue, the realm of essence corresponds roughly to the infinite number of possible worlds of which Leibniz speaks, while the realm of truth matches the one existing universe if viewed from the standpoint of its total history.

Such a notion of objective truth seems to separate Santayana from Wittgenstein in a final and definitive way. For Santayana, the realm of truth consists of the sum total of essences that characterize the march of time; it is, as he says, "the wake the ship of time plows upon the face of essence" (*SAF*, p. 227). This infinite totality of eternal forms is surely anathema to Wittgenstein, who wishes to speak neither of totality nor of the eternal. He sees only an open-ended multiplicity of language-games that cannot receive the closure needed for totality. And, he might remark, how could the truth be independent of what we think, if "truth" is a word in our language?

This momentous difference is, however, more apparent than real. To see the underlying deep commonality of view, we need to take a closer look at what Santayana says. A cursory first reading of his paean to truth misses the ironic subtext that undercuts what looks like an earnest effort to secure an objective matrix for our opinions. On a more careful examination, both totality and objectivity recede into the distance. Although Santayana speaks of the truth about any fact as comprehensive and of the realm of truth as an infinitely extended single domain, he always adds that neither can be encompassed by any mind. Opinions repeat only a small part of the truth about anything, and the totality of the realm of truth is but a speculative projection or background without vital connection to inquiry.

Even more remarkably, the truth includes every perspective generated by taking any fact "as a centre and viewing everything else only in relation with it" (*SAF*, p. 267). This makes all perceptions true, so long as we take into account the relational situation of the person perceiving. How, then, can we distinguish objective truth from subjective falsity, and how can we tell that the opinions we entertain are true? Those are matters of actual inquiry guided by the purposes of living animals. The practices of which inquiry consists determine what we are justified in calling true and what must be discarded as misleading or as false. The only functional distinction between truth and falsity derives, therefore, from our practices, the success of which constitutes the best and only adequate guide to what is true.

Stressing this side of Santayana's view evaporates the difference between the positions of our two philosophers. Wittgenstein also believes that truth is a function of the practices of which our form of life consists. The important insight they share is that truth is not a matter of subjective whim and that individuals are surrounded by social and natural realities they did not create and may not be able to change. Santayana and Wittgenstein agree that the world is independent of us, that much of it is not responsive to our needs, and that our dealings with it and our inquiries into it are all social. The significance of the accord is enhanced if we recall that Santayana claims no more than that his categories constitute "one of many languages in which the nature of things may be described" (*RB*, p. 453).

Santayana is convinced that there is an element of irreducible subjectivity in the world. He calls this consciousness, or spirit. He expands the notion to a *realm* of spirit to accommodate the possibility that there are different forms or different sorts of internal light associated with living matter. Spirit consists of diaphanous acts directed upon objects. The objects are always essences, the acts are evanescent moments of awareness generated by living organisms in the act of dealing with the world. These acts are private at least in the sense that no one has access to anyone else's subjectivity. But more, we cannot say anything about the intentional acts of awareness of which spirit consists beyond the recognition that they are moments of

Conclusion

vision, of intellectual synthesis. For the rest, we can discuss only the objects upon which such moments of consciousness open—the acts are truly transparent.

Without the realm of spirit, the world would consist only of matter in motion. The presence of consciousness is both a great gain and a vast loss in Santayana's view. The gain is that existence is able to acquire a vision, even if not an understanding, of itself. The loss is that reflection and awareness open the possibility of suffering. With suffering come the values, and the language, of good and evil, along with the possibility of transcending care for the fortunes of the animal in the form of the spiritual life. Spirituality consists of focusing on the immediacy of essence, removing thereby the worries natural to animals surrounded by threatening forces in the material world. Liberation from care is a natural outcome of the infinitely distant perspective spirit takes of what surrounds it.

The ineliminability of mind in terms of which Santayana expresses his view of spirit can be taken to imply a dualism. But we must be careful not to be misled about the sort of dualism involved. It is not any of the substance or attribute dualisms that have flourished since the days of Descartes. His notorious epiphenomenalism is more aptly describable as a residuum-dualism, meaning that even though mind lacks a causal role in the processes of the world, it cannot be converted into or eliminated in favor of any other reality. The integrity of consciousness cannot be abridged; in spite of its connection to the physical organism, its mode of being is different from that of the psyche.

This dogged and wholesome insistence that the subjective cannot be reduced to something else in echoed by Wittgenstein. If rejecting all attempts to reduce the mental to the physical makes one a dualist, then, surprising as this may sound, we must view Wittgenstein as a dualist also. Naturally his "dualism" does not take the form of an ontological position, but rather of the rejection of the project of forcing a monism upon us. In other words, he too is a residuum-dualist in the sense that he thinks subjectivity or the mental constitutes an irreducible residue in our lives, a surplus beyond the events science is in a position to catalogue and explain.[11]

This point is greatly bolstered by two additional considerations. The first is a related agreement between the two thinkers. They are at one in believing, stated in Wittgenstein's terms, that the language of mind is not part of any causally explanatory hypothesis to be evaluated by scientific criteria. The function of the language of sensations and intentions is altogether different from that of language-games in which we try to explain one or another set of events in the course of the world. Just as Wittgenstein rejects the attempt to reduce religious discourse to primitive science, so he would resist efforts to translate the language of mental events into the causal terms proper to experiment and explanation.

The second consideration is that, contrary to what one might suppose, Wittgenstein never denies the existence of sensations and other mental states. Rather he is at great pains to reject a certain model of the relation between sensation language and the facts which it expresses. He says, "if we construe the grammar of the expression of sensation on the model of 'object' and 'designation' the object drops out of consideration as irrelevant" (*PI*, 293). What is under attack here is not the reality of pain but a certain philosophy of language and its account of the language of sensations. Wittgenstein goes out of his way to distinguish between feeling pain and feigning pain (*PI*, 296). His intention is never to reject the existence of events we normally call mental, but to question the usual philosophical theories about the way such mental acts as thinking and believing are related to the use of language.

For Santayana, the significance of subjectivity is primarily moral in the broad sense of the term in which it refers to human flourishing. The spiritual dimension of mind affords us, in his view, quiet privacy and a certain distance from the world. This removal from our daily practices, from engagement with the problems of the moment, opens the skylight to transcendent joy. The vision of the infinite fields of eternity it presents is the stuff of philosophy as practiced by Spinoza and Schopenhauer.

Although Santayana does not think that spirituality is a necessary component of the good life for humans, he accords it high marks for the peace it showers on its practitioners. Philosophical reflection can

Conclusion

foster transcendent joy, and spirit, in turn, provides a refuge for philosophy or at least a place from which the thinker can cultivate the inner life of vision. Santayana reaffirms, in this way, the possibility of a real, even if modest, transcendence. The contact with the eternal yields no knowledge but it confers other benefits, including the satisfactions of seeing things whole and, from a great distance, seeing the whole of things.

The claim that such transcendence is possible and the intimate relation of philosophy to it constitutes a major difference between Santayana and Wittgenstein. The Wittgenstein of the *Tractatus* was clearly in love with grand vision.[12] Though he maintained that transcendent perspectives cannot be expressed in words, his crystalline description of his system suggests that he was in immediate possession of the whole of it. The rejection of the views of the *Tractatus* was at once a repudiation of the possibility of vision and a loss of interest in totality.

In his later work, accordingly, Wittgenstein has nothing to say about matters of cosmic or transcendent significance. He views the drive for vision of the whole of things as one of the great sources of philosophical error, and he leaves no positive or constructive task for the philosopher to undertake. If people wish to cultivate the inner life, they may do so. But thinking that such pursuits add anything to philosophy or that philosophy can make a contribution to them is to be lamentably deceived. The job of philosophy is to let the fly out of the fly-bottle, to lead us back to our piecemeal, sensible, ordinary practices, and thereby to allay even the desire for something grander or more.

Disagreement about what philosophy can or cannot do is at the center at what separates Santayana from Wittgenstein. Many, though not all, their other significant differences can be led back to their divergent assessments of the worth of philosophy. Since they are generally perceived as worlds apart, we have spent little time detailing their differences; showing their overlooked and surprising similarities beckoned to us as a task more interesting and more productive. But we cannot close without focusing on a structuring difference connected not with their evaluation of philosophy but with their diverse ways of doing it.

We have noted on several occasions that Wittgenstein's and Santayana's modes of philosophical reflection are profoundly at variance with one another. This difference in style expresses their beliefs about what philosophy can and ought to do and is therefore inseparable from the substance of their thought. The open-ended, multivoiced, herky-jerky character of Wittgenstein's writing is both a direct result and an effective instrument of his refusal to allow the philosophical enterprise to take wing. In the preface to *Philosophical Investigations* he writes: "After several unsuccessful attempts to weld my results into . . . a whole, I realized that I should never succeed. The best that I could write would never be more than philosophical remarks; my thoughts were soon crippled if I tried to force them on in any single direction against their natural inclination.— And this was, of course, connected with the very nature of the investigation" (vii).

The investigation aims to liberate us from the shackles of philosophical ways of thinking. What holds us captive is a picture or series of pictures—a vision, for instance, of how the world is or how language operates. Wittgenstein knew the power of images by reflecting on the picture of the world that had enthralled him when he wrote the *Tractatus* and on the central role the notion of picture plays in that work. The hold such images have on us must be broken, he thinks, but in such a way that no new vision takes their place. Accordingly he writes with the aim of denying pictures the opportunity to establish themselves or to gain dominance in the mind; he wishes to raise no philosophical edifice, and he wants none left intact upon the completion of his work.

This means that there are no unique philosophical tasks to accomplish, only various temptations to avoid. Wittgenstein wishes neither to advance views nor to counter prior philosophical theses with his own. Since he avoids such enterprises, he cannot *complete* his work; he can only halt his activity. "The real discovery," he says, "is the one that makes me capable of stopping doing philosophy . . ." (*PI*, 133). When one has done enough is unclear and perhaps arbitrary; the important consideration is that philosophy be done as a performance that leaves nothing at its conclusion.

Conclusion

Santayana, by contrast, writes having a completed vision in mind and with the purpose of conveying it. He presents sketch after sketch of the distinctions in terms of which his picture of the world is articulated. His descriptions of even the most mundane matters reflect, as does a microcosm, the structure of reality as he conceives it. Even though his categories are framed in irony and his language is that of a poet, he offers a picture of human beings caught in the flux of time, seeking liberation in eternity. He uses the terms of the great Western tradition of philosophy, and, much as he attenuates their meaning by employing them symbolically, he still thinks that their purpose is to guide life by focusing our minds on "the morally relevant facts" (*RB*, p. xi).

Insistence that his philosophy is personal, asking no "one to think in my terms if he prefers others," and that it is not one that encompasses the totality of things, placing him "at the heart of the universe" or at its origin, succeeds in differentiating it from the ambitious though futile adventures of traditional thought (*SAF*, pp. vi, v–vi). But Santayana's efforts still yield a product, a grand vision of what is important for the health of the soul. Moving transcendence from the sphere of metaphysical reality to the virtual realm of values—from immortality and actual communion with God to moments of carefree joy before we die—distances him from the substance of traditional philosophy but not from its final aim.

Which of these ways of appropriating and rejecting the tradition is preferable? Such questions have no definitive answers. At a philosophical level each has its serious limitations. Wittgenstein has been dismissed as having no philosophical position at all, and as we have seen Santayana has been reviled for merely warming over the tradition. On the other hand, Santayana has been accused of being too much of a poet and thus lacking philosophical rigor while Wittgenstein has been accused of being deliberately vague and difficult. At the same time each way has its strengths. Santayana, by speaking with the tradition, makes clear what his concerns are in the language of philosophy itself. Wittgenstein, by explicitly breaking with the tradition, forces his readers to a level of reflection that cannot easily fall into traditional patterns.[13]

This line of investigation brings the ultimate difference between Santayana and Wittgenstein clearly in view. We might think of traditional philosophers as architects attempting to build small replicas of the vault of heaven or accurate representations of the structure of reality. By comparison with them, Santayana is a painter creating a picture that symbolizes his situation and his mood, and that may be put to some use in pursuing the purposes of life. Wittgenstein, by contrast, is a musician whose performance evaporates in the act. The sounds, the moves, the licks delight or relieve or perhaps even liberate us, but they leave only silence when they stop. The painter aims to create a helpful or a beautiful product; the musician is fulfilled in the doing and demands neither literal nor symbolic representative value for his efforts.

If we view the movement from the metaphor of the architect to the metaphor of the musician in historical terms, we gain an insight into what has happened to philosophy in the last few hundred years. How we assess this development is determined at least partly by our own values and by our hopes for this field of endeavor. Wittgenstein has had a far greater impact on contemporary philosophy than has Santayana, and there seems to be a steady stream of people who think that philosophy is something we do to remedy the mistakes of the past or that it is something soon no one will do.

But the final chapter about philosophy and about the ambitions of these two thinkers for their field has not yet been written. The influence they will exercise on coming generations depends on how those who are students now and those as yet unborn will view the promise of reflection on the baffling, ambiguous condition of humans in the world. This places the future of Santayana and of Wittgenstein in the hands of their successors. And we all know that the fate of philosophers in the hands of their interpreters is impossible to predict.

Notes

CHAPTER ONE: THINKING IN THE RUINS

1. See John Dewey, *The Quest for Certainty*, ed. Jo Ann Boydston, intro. Stephen Toulmin (Carbondale: Southern Illinois University Press, 1994). chapter 1.

2. See, for example, the opening sections of Wittgenstein's *Culture and Value*, ed. G. H. von Wright, trans. P. Winch (Oxford: Basil Blackwell, 1980).

3. Although we will not explicitly address Saul Kripke's arguments that Wittgenstein in fact invented a powerful new form of skepticism, we present a very different, nonskeptical Wittgenstein; see Saul Kripke, *On Rules and Private Language* (Cambridge, Mass.: Harvard University Press, 1982).

4. This is not to suggest that Nietzsche's philosophical significance is limited to the negative project of bringing modern philosophy to an end. As will be evident in what follows, his work contributed greatly to another form of response to the discovery of contingency.

5. Ludwig Wittgenstein, *Tractatus Logico-Philosophicus*, trans. D. F. Pears and B. F. McGuiness (London: Routledge & Kegan Paul, 1961); and Ludwig Wittgenstein, *Philosophical Investigations*, 2d ed., trans. G. E. M. Anscombe (Oxford: Basil Blackwell, 1958).

6. This indictment treats the tendency to fall into philosophical confusion as a kind of sickness. See James Peterman, *Philosophy as Therapy: An Interpretation and Defense of Wittgenstein's Later Philosophical Project* (Albany: SUNY Press, 1992).

7. Ludwig Wittgenstein, *Remarks on Frazer's Golden Bough* in *Philosophical Occasions*, ed. James C. Klagge and Alfred Nordmann (Indianapolis: Hacket Publishing Co., 1993).

8. This insistence on difference, this refusal to reduce one form of human activity to another, is characteristic of the later Wittgenstein and is a commitment he shares with Santayana. Of course, each justifies it in a different way.

9. These themes will be developed in more detail in chapter 5.

10. For further discussion of the place of language games, see the classic piece by Rush Rhees, "Wittgenstein's Builders," *Proceedings of the Aristotelian Society,* 1959–1960.

11. The similarity to Santayana on this point is obvious and will be discussed below.

12. It is not clear whether the deferral and interruption that are characteristic of postmodern thought are meant to serve the purpose of eventual constructive transformation or to stand on their own. If the former, they become a strategic moment in a larger pragmatic project. Only in the latter case do they constitute a distinctive response to contingency, a response that consists of embracing it, of reminding us of it, and of articulating its details.

13. See Richard Rorty, *Contingency, Irony and Solidarity* (Cambridge: Cambridge University Press, 1989), p. 73.

14. Rorty, *Contingency,* chapters 2–3.

15. Richard Rorty, "The Priority of Democracy to Philosophy," in *Reading Rorty,* ed. Alan Malachowski (Oxford: Basil Blackwell, 1990).

16. Rorty, *Contingency,* p. 192.

17. John Stuhr, *Genealogical Pragmatism* (Albany: State University of New York Press, 1997); and Simon Critchley, "Deconstruction and Pragmatism—Is Derrida a Private Ironist or a Public Liberal," in *Deconstruction and Pragmatism,* ed. Chantal Mouffe (New York: Routledge, 1996).

CHAPTER TWO: ANIMAL FAITH AND FORMS OF LIFE

1. Ludwig Wittgenstein, *On Certainty,* ed. G. E. M. Anscombe and G. H. von Wright, trans. Denis Paul and G. E. M. Anscombe (Oxford: Basil Blackwell, 1969).

2. We do not propose to argue for the adequacy of the interpretations of philosophers that we offer here. Scholarly detail is irrelevant to the task at hand. Even where our accounts are less than fully developed, they serve our purposes well enough.

3. And it is skepticism of a Humean sort that Kripke suggests is Wittgenstein's purpose.

4. For other discussions of Wittgenstein and epistemology, see Michael Williams, *Groundless Belief: An Essay on the Possibility of Epistemology* (New Haven: Yale University Press, 1977); and Marie McGinn,

Sense and Certainty: A Dissolution of Scepticism (Oxford: Basil Black-well, 1989).

5. Other discussions of Wittgenstein's closing the gap between minds and bodies include John Cooke, "Human Beings," in *Studies in the Philosophy of Wittgenstein,* ed. Peter Winch (London: Routledge & Kegan Paul, 1969); and Ilham Dilman, *Love and Human Separateness* (Oxford: Basil Blackwell, 1987), chapter 1.

6. Stanley Cavell takes up the issues of skepticism and Wittgenstein in terms of what he calls the ordinary and the everyday. See his *The Claim of Reason* (New York: Oxford University Press, 1979); also see *The Cavell Reader,* ed. Stephen Mulhall (Oxford: Basil Blackwell, 1996).

7. It is just this focus on the fundamental character of animal certainty as something that lies beyond justification that should put the reader in mind of Santayana's notion of animal faith, which he contrasts with skepticism.

8. See G. E. Moore, "Proof of an External World," *Proceedings of the British Academy,* vol. 25, 1939; also "A Defense of Common Sense" in *Contemporary British Philosophy,* 2d series, ed. J. H. Muirhead, 1925. Both papers are reprinted in Moore's *Philosophical Papers,* (London: Allen and Unwin, 1959; New York: Macmillan, 1959).

9. It might be suggested—following Descartes—that there is a particular doubt here. I might, after all, be dreaming. But is that true? Do I have any reason to believe that I am actually dreaming? How different would the world have to be for me reasonably to wonder if all of life is a dream? It is by no means clear that such a claim (without a specific context) constitutes a serious doubt at all. See the comments concerning Descartes below.

10. It is interesting to note Wittgenstein and Santayana's agreement that once the skeptic's question gets raised, there can be no adequate reply.

11. The duality suggested here sometimes takes the form of the supposed distinction between the semantics of a language and its mere pragmatics—the meanings of terms as opposed to the conditions of their use. Wittgenstein would reject the distinction in the form in which it would have to be developed to sustain the argument.

12. See Michael Hodges, *Transcendence and Wittgenstein's Tractatus* (Philadelphia: Temple University Press, 1990).

13. Wittgenstein's presentation of the issue here makes it clear that this skeptical notion of doubt is tied to a Cartesian view of mind as distanced from all "practical effects."

14. Wittgenstein makes the same point with regard to belief. See section 89 of *On Certainty*.

15. This point was brought home to us in this particular form by Kathleen E. Bohstedt's "Funny Knowledge Claims: Wittgenstein's Rejection of Skepticism," read at the Southern Society for Philosophy and Psychology, March 29, 1991, in Atlanta, Georgia.

16. We have in mind wholesale skepticism, such as one that draws a distinction between practical and methodological doubt, in order to isolate the latter and give it free rein. A skeptical attitude toward selected details of life does not impede action in general, only precipitous or unexamined action.

17. The burden of Santayana's argument in *Scepticism and Animal Faith* is that skepticism consistently maintained is incompatible with all belief and action. The skeptic is reduced to silent appreciation of essence.

18. See John Lachs, "Belief, Confidence and Faith," *Southern Journal of Philosophy* 10 (Summer 1972): 277–85.

19. This, in fact, is the title of chapter 7 of *Scepticism and Animal Faith*.

20. Wittgenstein makes much of this anomaly in his refusal to allow the project to get started; this is also the anomaly that convicts skepticism of "dishonesty" for Santayana.

21. *SAF*, p. vi.

22. C. S. Peirce, "The Fixation of Belief," in *Philosophical Writings of Peirce*, ed. Justus Buchler (New York: Dover, 1955), pp. 5–22.

23. On the connections between practical doubt and situated practices in Wittgenstein and Peirce, see Thomas Crocker, "Wittgenstein's Practices and Peirce's Habits: Agreement in Human Activity," *History of Philosophy Quarterly* 15 (October 1998): 475–93.

24. *PI*, 2, 6.

25. For further discussion of Wittgenstein's builders see Warren Goldfarb, "I Want You to Bring Me a Slab: Remarks on the Opening Sections of the *Philosophical Investigations*," *Synthese* 56 (September 1983): 265–82.

26. It should be remembered that at least twice Wittgenstein also makes reference to the animal as the basis or source of our living epistemic standards. See *On Certainty*, pp. 475 and 358–59, both sections quoted and discussed earlier.

CHAPTER THREE: THE CONTINGENCY OF VALUES

1. The pioneer in this area is James Edwards in his book *Ethics without Philosophy: Wittgenstein and the Moral Life* (Tampa: University Presses of

Florida, 1982). For further discussions of the ethical dimensions of Wittgenstein's thought, see Cora Diamond, *The Realistic Spirit* (Cambridge, Mass.: MIT Press, 1991), chapters 11 and 15; and D. Z. Phillips, *Intervention in Ethics* (London: Macmillan, 1992).

2. For Santayana morality is, similarly, structured by the values the human animal embraces in the course of its social operations. Without the concrete context provided by shared habits and individual preferences, morality could have neither content nor justification.

3. See Michael Hodges, "The Status of Ethical Judgments in the *Philosophical Investigations*," *Philosophical Investigations* 18 (April 1995): 99–112.

4. See Michael Hodges, *Transcendence and Wittgenstein's Tractatus* (Philadelphia: Temple University Press, 1990).

5. At a later point we will consider the fascinating question of whether or not there is a form of thinking that occupies the moment before the philosopher's trick and that might lay proper claim to the title "philosophy." A full assessment of the relation of his later philosophy to Santayana's inevitably raises the question of whether Wittgenstein's enterprise is indeed purely negative.

6. Wittgenstein points to such likenesses throughout *Philosophical Investigations* and calls attention to their relations to certain of our linguistic practices. See, for example, 142, 244, 249, 474, 480 and part 2, section 11, p. 226. There are many other examples in *Philosophical Investigations* as well as in *On Certainty* and *The Remarks on the Foundations of Mathematics*.

7. A fuller discussion of these points is found in chapter 8 of *Transcendence and Wittgenstein's Tractatus*. Of course the facts in question here are not Tractarian facts, but ordinary facts such as children burnt by fire fear it.

8. We are not suggesting that agreement in form of life is simply agreement in language used. Rather Wittgenstein seems to mean that agreement in form of life underlies and makes possible agreement in language used. We will say more about this shortly.

9. Santayana notes that human beings might be "so far apart in nature and ideals that, like men and mosquitoes, they can stand in physical relations only, and if they meet can meet only to poison or to crush one another." *Reason in Science* (New York: Collier, 1962), p. 158.

10. For an interesting discussion of Wittgenstein's philosophical therapy, see Judith Genova, *Wittgenstein: A Way of Seeing* (London: Routledge, 1995).

11. For further discussion of Wittgenstein's method, see S. Stephen Hilmy, *The Later Wittgenstein: The Emergence of a New Philosophical Method* (Oxford: Basil Blackwell, 1987).

12. On a straightforward representational reading, this demand for philosophical closure is definitive of the project of the *Tractatus*. Thus Wittgenstein argues that the world must have a substance—objects—because "if the world had no substance, then whether a proposition had sense would depend on whether another proposition were true. In that case we could not sketch out any picture of the world (true or false)" (*Tractatus*, 2.0211–2). The very attempt to gather up the "totality of propositions" would always leave some out of the picture.

13. Paul Johnston makes this point very well in his *Wittgenstein and Moral Philosophy* (New York: Routledge, 1989), p. 81.

14. This descriptive claim as to the social constitution of individuals must not be confused with such normative positions as communitarianism. For other discussions of Wittgenstein and social issues, see Hannah Pitkin, *Wittgenstein and Justice* (Berkeley: University of California Press, 1972); Charles Taylor, *Philosophical Arguments* (Cambridge, Mass.: Harvard University Press, 1995), especially chapter 9, "To Follow a Rule"; and Alasdair MacIntyre, *After Virtue* (Notre Dame, Ind.: University of Notre Dame Press, 1981).

15. There is an interesting parallel here with Santayana. Just as Wittgenstein rejects the idea that what is of interest to the philosopher is a causal hypothesis about the formation of moral and other concepts, so Santayana maintains that ethics deals not with causes but with "their fruits and begins where they end." (*Reason in Science*, p. 154). No doubt there are causes at work in the formation of human reactions, but ethics begins with those reactions, however formed, and attempts to work them into a coherent set.

16. A host of issues is brought into focus here. Why does Wittgenstein believe, if indeed he does, that concepts can be a function of our natural history but not of our social history? In what ways relevant to the issues Wittgenstein discusses can the two be separated, in any case? If, as Wittgenstein contends, "Commanding, questioning, recounting, chatting, are as much a part of our natural history as walking, eating, drinking, playing" (*PI*, 25), where does social history end and natural history begin?

17. This is not an altogether implausible claim, for many in the American philosophical tradition would take hold of the insight in this evaluative way. For Dewey and others in that tradition, an imaginative awareness of possibility is a condition of intelligent, transformative action. Thus to the

extent that we come to see it as one among various possibilities and not as completely "filling the space of possibility," any current practice takes on an optionality and opens to transformation.

18. There is significant evidence that Wittgenstein would take this attitude. Consider, for example, his treatment of religious belief in *Culture and Value* and in *Remarks on Frazer's Golden Bough*. His attempts to disentangle religious practice from metaphysical/historical claims on the one hand and pseudoscience on the other aim at "leaving religion alone." If anything, one can detect in him an admiration for the wisdom of long-standing human practices, many of which he wants to protect from the irrelevant demands of philosophy.

19. One need not assume that such a task can be completed in a once-and-for-all fashion. We are calling attention only to the fact that Wittgenstein thinks the sole task of philosophy is that of gaining a "clear view of our use of words." It has no other positive role. Indeed Wittgenstein repeatedly attempted to persuade his students to return to other human practices and abandon philosophical pursuits, sometimes with tragic results. See Ray Monk, *Wittgenstein: The Duty of Genius* (New York: Free Press, 1990).

20. *SAF*, p. 1

21. At *PI*, 66 and following, Wittgenstein discusses the way in which differences underlie the sameness imposed by language.

22. George Santayana, *Physical Order and Moral Liberty*, ed. John Lachs and Shirley Lachs (Nashville: Vanderbilt University Press, 1969), p. 196.

23. *RB*, p. 483.

CHAPTER FOUR: FORMS OF LIFE AND ANIMAL FAITH

1. On interpreting "forms of life," see David Pears, *Wittgenstein* (London: Fontana Press, 1971); and Richard Rorty, "Keeping Philosophy Pure: An Essay on Wittgenstein," in his *Consequences of Pragmatism* (Minneapolis: University of Minnesota Press, 1982).

2. The obvious exceptions to this claim do not falsify it. Of course one might break a leg playing ball or might even be killed. And some athletes make livings from the game, which clearly endows it with significance beyond its narrow confines. Nonetheless a game in this sense is still an isolated activity. It does not fit seamlessly into the wider context of our activities as, say, building houses and eating do.

3. We must be careful not to speak of "the world" here in anything like a Tractarian sense, as "the totality of facts," for such a conception presupposes the very transcendence that the later Wittgenstein intends to displace.

4. We saw a particularly clear example of this in our discussion of Wittgenstein's treatment of skepticism in chapter 2.

5. We have already noted various places where Wittgenstein appeals to the animal-like character of human practices. For more on understanding and forms of life, see Peter Winch, "Understanding a Primitive Society," *American Philosophical Quarterly* 1 (October 1964): 307–24; and Charles Taylor, "Understanding and Ethnocentricity," in his *Philosophy and the Human Sciences: Philosophical Papers,* vol. 2 (Cambridge: Cambridge University Press, 1985).

6. Linear B was not translated until the 1950s. Here the problem was simply a matter of ability to decipher what was clearly a language, but one that we did not have enough information to translate. Such problems may remain unsolved for a time but the accumulation of knowledge eventually enables us to master them.

7. Newton Garver's interesting book, *This Complicated Form of Life* (La Salle: Open Court Press, 1994), develops Wittgenstein's thought from this particular passage.

8. It has been suggested that Wittgenstein is just wrong about hope. What of the dog that sits expectantly by the table in hopes of getting a scrap of food? But that there are such relatively simple cases does not cut against the thrust of the point here.

9. *PI,* no. 127.

10. *RB,* pp. 202–3.

Chapter 5: Religious Belief

1. For a systematic exposition of Wittgenstein's views in relation to theology, see Fergus Kerr, *Theology after Wittgenstein* (Oxford: Basil Blackwell, 1986).

2. Rush Rhees, *Ludwig Wittgenstein, Personal Recollections* (Totowa, N.J.: Rowman and Littlefield, 1981), p. 108.

3. Rush Rhees, *Without Answers* (New York: Shocken Books, 1969), p. 121.

4. To maintain that it is unique is not to say that, in the pursuit of particular purposes, we cannot usefully compare it to various other human activities. It does, however, involve denial of the legitimacy of any

reductionist project that claims religion is nothing but something else in disguise.

5. Since history and science make no religious claims, they offer nothing for religion to assess. It is, of course, possible for devout people to condemn a consuming interest in science if it interferes with attention to religious duties.

6. See Peter Winch, *The Idea of a Social Science* (London: Routledge & Kegan Paul, 1958).

7. George Santayana, *The Idea of Christ in the Gospels* (New York: C. Scribner's Sons, 1946), p. 4.

8. See E. Renan, *The Life of Jesus* (New York: Modern Library, 1927); and Albert Schweitzer, *The Quest for the Historical Jesus* (New York: Macmillan, 1948).

9. The same distinction is the founding idea of Santayana's *The Idea of Christ in the Gospels.*

10. D. Z. Phillips takes up these issues in his writings on Wittgenstein's views about religion. See, for example, *Wittgenstein and Religion* (New York: St. Martin's Press, 1993).

11. M. O'C. Drury, "Some Notes on Conversations with Wittgenstein," in *Ludwig Wittgenstein, Personal Recollections.* Ed. Rush Rhees (Totowa, N.J.: Rowman and Littlgefield, 1981), p. 94.

12. See Michael P. Hodges, "Transcendence, Genealogy and Reinscription," in *Religion without Transcendence?* Ed. D. Z. Phillips and Timothy Tessin (New York: St. Martin's Press, 1997), in which the author argues that Wittgenstein does not regard religious practice as immune to criticism.

13. George Santayana, *Interpretations of Poetry and Religion* (New York: C. Scribner's Sons, 1900); *The Idea of Christ in the Gospels.*

14. See Santayana's reinterpretation of the Nicene Creed in *Realms,* pp. 845–53.

CHAPTER SIX: CONCLUSION

1. Wittgenstein was aware of this and despaired of improvement at the same time as he contended that such "disorganization" was essential to his thought. See *PI,* preface, p. vii. We must also keep in mind that much of the later work was not prepared for publication by Wittgenstein.

2. *PI,* 19.

3. For one version of this position, see Bernard Williams, "Wittgenstein and Idealism," in his *Moral Luck* (Cambridge: Cambridge University Press, 1981).

Notes to Chapter Six

4. See M. P. Hodges, *Transcendence and Wittgenstein's Tractatus,* especially chapters 8–12.

5. One might argue that Wittgenstein has already developed this alternative in the early work.

6. "Some Meanings of the Word 'Is,'" in George Santayana, *Obiter Scripta,* ed. Justus Buchler and Benjamin Schwartz (New York: C. Scribner's Sons, 1936).

7. *SAF,* pp. 70–71.

8. Wittgenstein takes up necessity in *Remarks on the Foundations of Mathematics.* For further discussion, see the exchange between Michael Dummett and Barry Stroud in George Pitcher (ed.), *Wittgenstein: The Philosophical Investigations* (New York: Doubleday & Co., 1966).

9. *SAF,* p. 121.

10. There are a number of passages that make this point. See, for example, *Obiter Scripta,* pp. 110, 166.

11. For other discussions of Wittgenstein's eschewing the dualism/monism debate, see B. R. Tilghman, *Wittgenstein, Ethics and Aesthetics* (New York: SUNY Press, 1991), especially chapter 5, "Discerning Humanity"; and David Cockburn, *Other Human Beings* (London: Macmillan, 1990). Also see John Cooke's article, "Human Beings," in *Studies in the Philosophy of Wittgenstein,* ed. Peter Winch (London: Routledge & Kegan Paul, 1969).

12. This standard interpretation of the early Wittgenstein has been challenged in recent years by among others Cora Diamond. See her "Throwing Away the Ladder: How to Read the *Tractatus*" in *The Realistic Spirit* (Cambridge, Mass.: MIT Press, 1991).13. We say "easily" because many commentators persist in finding a variety of traditional philosophical claims in Wittgenstein's later work. At least all such interpretations must be at variance with Wittgenstein's own remarks.

Bibliography

Alexander, Thomas. "Santayana's Unbearable Lightness of Being: Aesthetics as a Prelude to Ontology," *Bulletin of the Santayana Society* II (Fall 1993): 1-10.

———."Santayana's Sage: The Disciplines of Aesthetic Enlightenment," *Transactions of the Charles S. Peirce Society* 33 (Spring 1997): 328-57.

Arnett, Willard. *Santayana and the Sense of Beauty* (Bloomington: Indiana University Press, 1957).

Bohstedt, Kathleen E. "Funny Knowledge Claims: Wittgenstein's Rejection of Skepticism," read at the Southern Society for Philosophy and Psychology, March 29, 1991, in Atlanta, Georgia.

Cavell, Stanley. *The Claim of Reason* (New York: Oxford University Press, 1979).

———. *The Cavell Reader,* ed. Stephen Mulhall (Oxford: Basil Blackwell, 1996).

Cockburn, David. *Other Human Beings* (London: Macmillan, 1990).

Cooke, John. "Human Beings," in *Studies in the Philosophy of Wittgenstein,* ed. Peter Winch (London: Routledge & Kegan Paul, 1969).

Critchley, Simon."Deconstruction and Pragmatism-Is Derrida a Private Ironist or a Public Liberal?" in *Deconstruction and Pragmatism,* ed. Chantal Mouffe (New York: Routledge, 1996).

Crocker, Thomas. "Wittgenstein's Practices and Peirce's Habits: Agreement in Human Activity," *History of Philosophy Quarterly* 15 (October 1998): 475-93.

Dewey, John. *Experience and Nature,* ed. Jo Ann Boydston, intro. Sidney Hook (Carbondale: Southern Illinois University Press, 1994).

———. *The Quest for Certainty,* ed. Jo Ann Boydston, intro. Stephen Toulmin (Carbondale: Southern Illinois University Press, 1994).

Diamond, Cora. *The Realistic Spirit* (Cambridge, Mass.: MIT Press, 1991).

Dilman, Ilham. *Love and Human Separateness* (Oxford: Basil Blackwell, 1987).

Edwards, James. *Ethics without Philosophy: Wittgenstein and the Moral Life* (Tampa: University Presses of Florida, 1982).[i]

Bibliography

Garver, Newton. *This Complicated Form of Life* (La Salle: Open Court Press, 1994).

Genova, Judith. *Wittgenstein: A Way of Seeing* (London: Routledge, 1995).

Goldfarb, Warren. "I Want You to Bring Me a Slab: Remarks on the Opening Sections of the *Philosophical Investigations,*" *Synthese* 56 (September 1983): 265-82.

Goodman, Russell. "What Wittgenstein Learned from William James," *History of Philosophy Quarterly* 11 (July 1994): 339-54.

Grossman, Morris. "Interpreting Interpretations," *Bulletin of the Santayana Society* 8 (Fall 1990): 18-28.

Hintikka, Jaakko, "Language Games," *Acta Philosophica Fennica,* 28 (1976): 105-125.

———, "Wittgenstein and the Problem of Phenomenology," *Acta Philosophica Fennica,* 49 (1990): 15-46.

Hilmy, S. Stephen. *The Later Wittgenstein: The Emergence of a New Philosophical Method* (Oxford: Basil Blackwell, 1987).

Hodges, Michael. *Transcendence and Wittgenstein's Tractatus* (Philadelphia: Temple University Press, 1990).

———. "The Status of Ethical Judgments in the *Philosophical Investigations,*" *Philosophical Investigations* 18 (April 1995): 99-112.

———. "Transcendence, Genealogy and Reinscription," in *Religion without Transcendence?* ed. D. Z. Phillips and Timothy Tessin (New York: St. Martin's Press, 1997).

Johnston, Paul. *Wittgenstein and Moral Philosophy* (New York: Routledge, 1989).

Kerr, Fergus. *Theology after Wittgenstein* (Oxford: Basil Blackwell, 1986).

Kerr-Lawson, Angus. "Essentialism and Santayana's Realm of Essence," *Transactions of the Charles S. Peirce Society* 21 (Spring, 1985): 200-21.

———. "Santayana's Non-Reductive *Naturalism,*" *Transactions of the Charles S. Peirce Society* 25 (Summer, 1989): 229-50.

———. "Pragmatism and Santayana's Realms," *Bulletin of the Santayana Society* 12 (Fall 1994): 17-21.

Kripke, Saul. *On Rules and Private Language* (Cambridge, Mass.: Harvard University Press, 1982).

Lachs, John. "Belief, Confidence and Faith," *Southern Journal of Philosophy* 10 (Summer 1972): 277-85.

———. *Mind and Philosophers* (Nashville: Vanderbilt University Press, 1987).

———. *George Santayana* (Boston: Twayne, 1988).

Bibliography

————. *The Relevance of Philosophy to Life* (Nashville: Vanderbilt University Press, 1995).

Levinson, Henry Samuel. *Santayana, Pragmatism, and the Spiritual Life* (Chapel Hill: University of North Carolina Press, 1991).

MacDonald, Douglas. "Santayana's Undivided Soul," *Southern Journal of Philosophy* 10 (Summer 1972): 237-52.

MacIntyre, Alasdair. *After Virtue* (Notre Dame, Ind.: University of Notre Dame Press, 1981).

Malcolm, Norman. *A Religious Point of View?* (Ithaca, N.Y.: Cornell University Press, 1995).

McGinn, Marie. *Sense and Certainty: A Dissolution of Scepticism* (Oxford: Basil Blackwell, 1989).

Monk, Ray. *Wittgenstein: The Duty of Genius* (New York: Free Press, 1990).

Moore, G. E. "Proof of an External World," *Proceedings of the British Academy,* vol. 25, 1939.

————. "A Defense of Common Sense" in *Contemporary British Philosophy, 2nd Series,* ed. J. H. Muirhead, 1925.

————. *Philosophical Papers* (London: Allen and Unwin), 1959.

Pears, David. *Wittgenstein* (London: Fontana Press, 1971).

Peirce, C. S. "The Fixation of Belief," in *Philosophical Writings of Peirce,* ed. Justus Buchler (New York: Dover, 1955).

Peterman, James. *Philosophy as Therapy: An Interpretation and Defense of Wittgenstein's Later Philosophical Project* (Albany: SUNY Press, 1992).

Phillips, D. Z. *Intervention in Ethics* (London: Macmillan, 1992).

————. *Wittgenstein and Religion* (New York: St. Martin's Press, 1993).

Pitcher, George (ed.). *Wittgenstein: The Philosophical Investigations* (New York: Doubleday & Co., 1966).

Pitkin, Hannah. *Wittgenstein and Justice* (Berkeley: University of California Press, 1972).

Renan, E. *The Life of Jesus* (New York: Modern Library, 1927).

Rhees, Rush. "Wittgenstein's Builders," *Proceedings of the Aristotelian Society,* 1959-1960.

————. *Without Answers* (New York: Shocken Books, 1969).

Rhees, Rush (ed.). *Ludwig Wittgenstein, Personal Recollections,* (Totowa, N.J. Rowman and Littlefield, 1981).

Rorty, Richard. "Keeping Philosophy Pure: An Essay on Wittgenstein," in his *Consequences of Pragmatism* (Minneapolis: University of Minnesota Press, 1982).

Bibliography

———. *Contingency, Irony and Solidarity* (Cambridge: Cambridge University Press, 1989), p. 73.

———. "The Priority of Democracy to Philosophy," in *Reading Rorty*, ed. Alan Malachowski (Oxford: Basil Blackwell, 1990).

Saatkamp, Herman J., and John Jones. *George Santayana: A Bibliographical Checklist, 1880-1980* (Bowling Green: Philosophy Documentation Center, 1982).

———. "Animal Faith," *Southern Journal of Philosophy* 10 (Summer 1972): 167-71.

Santayana, George. *The Works of George* Santayana, vol. 3, *Interpretations of Poetry and Religion*, ed. William G. Holzberger and Herman Saatkamp, intro. Joel Porte (first pub. in 1900; Cambridge, Mass.: MIT Press, 1989).

———. *The Life of Reason*, vol. 3: *Reason and Religion* (first pub. in 1905-1906; New York: Collier Books, 1962).

———. *The Life of Reason*, vol. 5: *Reason in Science* (New York: Collier, 1962).

———. *Scepticism and Animal Faith* (first pub. in 1923; New York: Dover, 1955).

———. *Realms of Being* (first pub. in 1925-1941; New York: Cooper Square, 1972).

———. *Winds of Doctrine* (New York: C. Scribner's Sons, 1926).

———. *Obiter Scripta*, ed. Justus Buchler and Benjamin Schwartz (New York: C. Scribner's Sons, 1936).

———. *The Idea of Christ in the Gospels* (New York: C. Scribner's Sons, 1946).

———. *Animal Faith and Spiritual Life*, ed. John Lachs (New York: Appleton-Century-Crofts, 1967).

———. *Physical Order and Moral Liberty*, ed. John Lachs and Shirley Lachs (Nashville: Vanderbilt University Press, 1969).

Schweitzer, Albert. *The Quest for the Historical Jesus* (New York: Macmillan, 1948).

Singer, Beth. *The Rational Society: A Critical Study of Santayana's Social Thought* (Cleveland: Case Western University Press, 1970).

Sprigge, Timothy. *Santayana* (New York: Routledge, 1995).

Stuhr, John. *Genealogical Pragmatism: Philosophy, Experience, and Community* (Albany: State University of New York Press, 1997).

Bibliography

Taylor, Charles. "Understanding and Ethnocentricity," in his *Philosophy and the Human Sciences: Philosophical Papers,* vol. 2 (Cambridge: Cambridge University Press, 1985).

———. *Philosophical Arguments* (Cambridge, Mass.: Harvard University Press, 1995).

Tilghman, B. R. *Wittgenstein, Ethics and Aesthetics* (New York: SUNY Press, 1991).

Williams, Bernard. "Wittgenstein and Idealism," in his *Moral Luck* (Cambridge: Cambridge University Press, 1981).

Williams, Michael. *Groundless Belief: An Essay on the Possibility of Epistemology* (New Haven: Yale University Press, 1977).

Winch, Peter. *The Idea of a Social Science* (London: Routledge & Kegan Paul, 1958).

———. "Understanding a Primitive Society," *American Philosophical Quarterly* 1 (October 1964): 307-24.

Wittgenstein, Ludwig. *Tractatus Logico-Philosophicus* (London: Routledge & Kegan Paul, 1961).

———. *Philosophical Investigations,* 2d ed., trans. G. E. M. Anscombe (Oxford: Basil Blackwell, 1958).

———. *Remarks on the Foundations of Mathematics,* 3d ed., ed. G. H. von Wright, Rush Rhees, G. E. M. Anscombe, trans. G. E. M. Anscombe (Oxford: Basil Blackwell, 1978).

———. *On Certainty,* ed. G. E. M. Anscombe and G. H. von Wright, trans. Denis Paul and G. E. M. Anscombe (Oxford: Basil Blackwell, 1969).

———. *Culture and Value,* ed. G. H. von Wright, trans. P. Winch (Oxford: Basil Blackwell, 1980).

———. *Remarks on Frazer's Golden Bough,* in *Philosophical Occasions,* ed. James C. Klagge and Alfred Nordmann (Indianapolis: Hacket Publishing Co., 1993).

———. *Lectures and Conversations on Aesthetics, Psychology and Religious Belief,* ed. Cyril Barrett (Oxford: Basil Blackwell, 1996).

Index

absolute, 7, 10, 15-17, 37
action, 6, 10, 18-20, 26, 27, 31, 34, 41, 49, 52, 66, 79, 83, 89, 90
aesthetic(s), 13, 42, 71
analytic philosophy, 87
animal, 10, 11, 13, 17-19, 32, 33, 43, 48, 52, 54, 55, 59, 60, 63-73, 84-86, 102, 103
animal faith, 9, 10, 33, 34, 65, 66, 82,
anthropology, 45, 70
architect, 108
argument, 8, 29, 31, 39, 62
Aristotle, 49, 88
art, 52
Augustine, 72
authority, 6, 71, 79, 81-85

beauty, 11, 93
belief, 8, 9, 12, 19, 23-29, 34, 46, 49, 52, 62, 64, 66, 70, 71-72, 76-78, 81, 83, 89, 92
biology, 70
Bradley, F. H., 1
builder, 32, 56, 88

Cartesian, 15-17
category, 28, 73, 100
certainty, 2-5, 7, 9-20, 23, 24, 28-34, 62-64, 77
change, 6, 58, 68-70, 76, 77, 94, 98

Christianity, 8, 70-72, 75, 81, 85
commitment, 34-35, 53, 66, 67, 75-81, 83, 90, 95
compulsion, 67-68
concept(s), 40, 41, 44, 45, 60, 61, 99
conscience, 8, 68
consciousness, 3, 4, 13, 28-29, 82, 84-86, 89, 102, 103
conservative, 7, 8, 65
content, 9, 35, 36, 77, 78, 81
context(s), 1, 3, 5, 11, 13, 14, 16-21, 24, 31, 32, 34, 46, 47, 49, 52-58, 62-67, 75, 90, 96, 97
Continental philosophy, 87
contingency, 2-7, 9-12, 14, 46, 96
convention(s), 22, 66
Creation, 75, 85, 98
Critchley, S., 13
criticism, 47, 70

democracy, 10, 12, 79, 94
Descartes, R., 2, 4, 17, 22, 27, 88, 103
description(s), 13, 23, 40, 42, 62, 74, 86, 95, 97, 100, 107
Dewey, J., 5, 6, 12
difference(s), 1, 29, 39, 48, 51, 56, 66-69, 74-77, 83-87, 89, 91-95, 97, 98, 101, 102, 105-108

Index

discourse, 40-44, 73, 80-83, 88, 95, 96, 100, 104
dogmatism, 50
doubt, 7, 16, 17, 18-32, 61, 64, 76
dualism, 72, 103
dynamism, 98-99

Einstein, A., 16
empirical, 39, 45, 48, 71, 81, 82
ends, 3, 64
Enlightenment, 6, 12
epiphenomenalism, 103
epistemology, 41
essence, 10, 11, 13, 23, 69, 75, 80, 82, 86, 88, 93-103
ethics, 41-43, 46, 47
evidence, 17, 70, 72, 76, 78-79
evolution, 75
evolutionist, 70
existence, 18, 28-31, 33, 34, 57, 68, 82, 83 89, 93-98, 103, 104
existential, 64, 65
existentialist, 51
explanation, 68, 71, 73, 74, 98, 100, 104

fact(s), 28, 37, 39, 62, 72, 86, 89, 100-102
fact (matters of), 72, 81
faith, 1, 66, 71, 72, 76-79, 85
family resemblance, 12, 50, 97
finitude, 32
form(s), 4, 30, 55, 70, 94, 95, 98-101
form of life, 8, 17-19, 25, 26, 36-44, 53, 55-65, 67-69, 72-74, 90, 102
foundation, 2-9, 15, 17-19, 30, 37, 46, 61, 65, 67, 78, 90

foundationalist, 12, 37, 41
framework, 87
Frazer, J. G., 8, 73

game, 8, 17, 18, 20, 23-26, 31, 56, 62, 96
given, the, 27, 28, 30, 41, 60
goals, 93
God, 4, 28, 72, 75, 85, 86, 107
Gospels, 8, 76-78
grammar, 43, 44, 74, 104
ground, 61, 62, 65, 67, 84

history, 8, 46, 50, 72, 73, 75, 79, 86, 94, 101. *See also* natural history
history of philosophy, 47, 89
honesty, 31, 33, 63
human being, 26, 37-39, 57, 58, 67, 70, 71, 92, 101, 107
Hume, D., 16, 26, 28
Husserl, E., 28
Huxley, T. H., 70

ideal, 32, 47, 48, 50, 78-84
identity, 92, 98
idiom, 87-90, 97
impulse(s), 48, 53, 83, 84
individuals, 43-45, 47-51, 94, 102
inquiry, 31, 32, 38, 39, 64, 101-102
intellectual assent, 72, 76-79, 83
irony, 11-13, 88, 107

Jesus, 72, 75, 77-79
Judaism, 70
justification, 2, 3, 6, 9, 25, 34, 36, 42, 59, 63, 74, 90

Index

knowledge, 2, 3, 7, 9, 15-33, 35-37, 50, 64, 65, 68, 82, 91, 99, 105

language, 4, 9, 11, 17, 19, 23-25, 32, 36, 37, 39-41, 44, 46, 52, 55-60, 63-67, 72-77, 80, 87-93, 95-104, 106, 107

language-game, 8, 18, 20-26, 32, 33, 43, 53-57, 61-65, 73, 79, 95-101, 104

legitimacy, 7, 10, 11, 23, 33, 64, 65, 69, 79, 89, 100

Leibniz, G. W., 88, 96

liberalism, 12

limit(s), 18, 30, 65, 99

lion, 58-59

logic, 19, 37, 39, 88

magic(al), 72, 85

material, 27, 48, 82, 83, 88, 103

materialism, 100

mathematics, 46, 57, 75

matter, 82, 84, 85, 88, 93, 98, 99-102

meaning(s), 18, 24-25, 30, 36, 37, 38, 39, 42, 56, 58, 61-63, 72, 74, 95, 99, 100

mental, 49, 103-104

metaphysics, 72, 93

method, 15, 25, 33, 38, 42, 46, 57, 85, 91

mind, 17, 24, 27, 29, 52, 67, 86, 89, 96, 101-104

modern malaise, 2, 3

Monet, C., 45

monism, 103

Moore, G. E., 20-22, 42

moral/morality, 1, 3, 10, 28, 35, 39-41, 44, 46-53, 81, 88, 94, 101, 104

musician, 108

Napoleon, 76

natural, 32, 40, 60, 61, 84, 90, 96, 103

natural history, 40, 46, 58, 90, 95, 98

nature, 34, 41, 44-47, 49, 51, 85, 90, 99

necessity, 2, 4, 67, 95, 96

Nietzsche, F., 4

nihilist, 4

nonsensical, 62, 64, 73, 80

normativity, 35, 39

number, 38, 94, 96

object, 13, 15, 16, 23, 29, 30, 32, 34, 43, 78, 91, 94, 95, 102-104

objectivity, 91, 101

ontology, 13, 88-92

organism, 48-52, 83-85, 102, 103

orthodoxy, 9, 34, 66

painter, 108

Peirce, C. S., 31, 66

perception, 82, 84, 89, 102

philosophy, 2, 4, 7-12, 17, 31, 33-36, 41, 46, 47, 50, 51, 55, 63, 65-69, 75, 80, 81, 87-89, 93, 95, 100, 104-108

physics, 70, 79

pictorial, 82

picture, 6, 16-19, 36, 42, 45, 57, 75, 77, 80, 106-108

Plato, 2, 88, 94

postmodern(ism), 5, 6, 8, 11, 12, 14, 89, 100

practical, 78, 86

practical doubt, 16, 17, 22, 23, 31

Index

practices, 1-12, 21, 25-27, 31-37, 40-42, 44, 46, 47, 50, 52-58, 60-69, 73, 74, 90-92, 100-105
pragmatism, 5, 9, 14
preference, 36, 44, 48, 84
proposition(s), 19, 23, 28-30, 76, 78-80
psyche, 48, 51-53, 82-85, 103
psychology, 45, 98
purposes, 32, 35, 48, 53, 64, 84, 88, 95, 102, 108

reality, 4, 17, 29, 30, 65, 82, 90, 92, 95-96, 100, 103, 104, 107, 108
realm of essence, 10, 13, 94-101
realm of spirit, 102, 103
realm of truth, 100, 101
realms of being, 34, 91-93
reason, 7, 8, 39-43, 53, 68, 77, 79
reductionism, 71, 96
reductionist, 74
relation, 3, 13, 18, 20, 21, 30, 44, 45, 52, 56, 58, 75, 77-82, 88, 91, 92, 94-96, 98, 99, 102, 104, 105
relationalism (individual), 49-53
relativism, 37, 49
religion, 8, 70-75, 80-6, 97
reminders, 7, 41, 66, 99
Renan, E., 76
Rhees, R., 72
Rorty, R., 11-13
rules, 4, 40, 96

Sartre, Jean-Paul, 1
Schopenhauer, A., 104
Schweitzer, A., 76
science, 8, 45, 68, 70-75, 81-85, 97, 99, 103, 104
selectivity, 48, 84, 86, 96

self, 13, 28, 48, 84-85
self-identity, 28, 30, 94
sensations, 104
silence, 9, 27, 35, 91, 108
similarity, 38, 69, 87, 91, 95, 97
situated/situatedness, 3, 6, 11, 13, 21, 33, 35, 36, 40, 41, 47, 56, 57, 61, 64, 72, 90, 91, 96
skeptic, 16, 17, 20-22, 25-30, 91
skepticism, 2, 3, 9, 16, 17, 20, 26, 27, 30-32, 34, 35, 76
social, 1, 3, 5, 6, 13, 32, 40, 44, 47, 51-53, 58, 64, 66, 90, 96, 102
solipsism, 10, 27
soul, 48, 50, 52, 54, 71, 82-84, 92, 93, 107
spectator, 86
Spinoza, B., 88, 104
spirit, 4, 17, 33, 84-89, 93, 102-104
spiritual life, 10, 11, 13, 69, 103
stoic, 8, 11, 41
Stuhr, J., 13
subject, 29, 30
subjectivity, 102-104
substance, 67, 69, 88, 103
superstition, 71, 75
symbolic, 68, 71, 82, 94, 99, 108
system, 10, 33, 58, 59, 67, 78, 88, 105

thinking, 5, 11, 16, 25, 35, 36, 44, 62, 87, 89, 91, 104, 106
thought, 2, 4, 7, 12, 27, 29, 31, 38, 55, 60, 67, 73
time, 22, 68, 73, 76, 94, 101, 107,
totality, 6, 30, 36, 42, 47, 90, 91, 97, 101, 105, 107
tradition, 2, 3, 15, 28, 64, 74, 80, 86, 88, 89, 90, 107

Index

transcendence, 10, 11, 36, 37, 39, 40, 69, 93, 105, 107

transcendent, 9, 17, 18, 23, 53, 62, 73, 81, 104, 105

transcendental, 4, 47, 55

truth, 18, 33, 37, 61-68, 71, 75, 77, 78, 81, 89, 93, 96, 100-102

understanding, 18, 33, 35, 45, 49, 55, 56, 59, 62, 65, 68, 70, 72, 75, 77, 84, 89, 90, 99, 103

universal, 8, 33, 35, 47-50, 52, 53, 77, 92

universals, 88, 94

value, 5, 15, 33, 35, 36, 43, 44, 47, 48, 50, 51, 53, 89, 97, 108

Washington, G., 77

Michael P. Hodges is professor of philosophy and chair of the department at Vanderbilt University. He has written widely on Wittgenstein, including the book *Transcendence and Wittgenstein's Tractatus* (1990).

John Lachs is Centennial Professor of Philosophy at Vanderbilt University. Among his many publications are *George Santayana* (1988) and *In Love with Life: Reflections on the Joy of Living and Why We Hate to Die* (1998).